Fit Financial Approach

FIT
FINANCIAL APPROACH

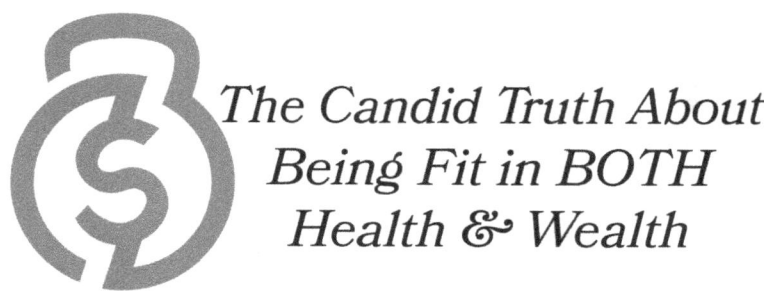

The Candid Truth About Being Fit in BOTH Health & Wealth

MIKE BROKER, CFP®, CPT

NEW YORK
LONDON • NASHVILLE • MELBOURNE • VANCOUVER

Fit Financial Approach
The Candid Truth About Being Fit in Both Health & Wealth

© 2021 Mike Broker, CFP®, CPT

All rights reserved. No portion of this book may be reproduced, stored in a retrieval system, or transmitted in any form or by any means—electronic, mechanical, photocopy, recording, scanning, or other—except for brief quotations in critical reviews or articles, without the prior written permission of the publisher.

Published in New York, New York, by Morgan James Publishing. Morgan James is a trademark of Morgan James, LLC. www.MorganJamesPublishing.com

ISBN 9781631954405 paperback
ISBN 9781631954412 eBook
Library of Congress Control Number: 2020950774

A FREE ebook edition is available for you or a friend with the purchase of this print book.

CLEARLY SIGN YOUR NAME ABOVE

Instructions to claim your free ebook edition:
1. Visit MorganJamesBOGO.com
2. Sign your name CLEARLY in the space above
3. Complete the form and submit a photo of this entire page
4. You or your friend can download the ebook to your preferred device

Cover & Interior Design by:
Christopher Kirk
www.GFSstudio.com

Morgan James is a proud partner of Habitat for Humanity Peninsula and Greater Williamsburg. Partners in building since 2006.

Get involved today! Visit
MorganJamesPublishing.com/giving-back

To Dexter, Callen, and Greta

Find your passion and follow it wherever it leads

TABLE OF CONTENTS

Acknowledgments ix
Preface xi
Broker-Dealer Disclosure. xiii
HEALTH & WEALTH 1
  A Symbiotic Relationship 1
  The Fit Financial Formula. 5
  Cutting Through the Misinformation 11
PILLARS OF PROGRESS 31
  Mindset. 31
  Planning 47
  Habits 69
EDUCATION 87
  Fundamental Truisms 87
  Cash & Calorie Flow. 96
  Net Worth & The Body 122

- Measuring Progress ... 147
- Protection for Your Plan ... 163
- Leaving a Legacy ... 179
- Hiring Professional Help ... 191

LIFE PHASES ... 201
- Getting Started ... 201
- Mid-Career ... 206
- Pre-Retirement ... 210
- Retirement ... 214

TOOL KIT ... 219
- FitFinancial Test™ ... 219
- Quick Fixes ... 221

CONCLUSION ... 229
ABOUT THE AUTHOR ... 231
Common Questions & Misconceptions ... 233

ACKNOWLEDGMENTS

Fit Financial Approach has been an endeavor many years in the making. Many people have supported me, supplied stories, and directly impacted the final product of this work. I have gleaned most of this book's information from direct work with clients in both fitness and wealth through the years. Without my fantastic clients making the choices that improve their lives one step at a time, this project would not exist.

My editor Elizabeth Bartasius helped me find my written voice while turning an unorganized mess of ideas into a readable, coherent book. Her patience with me, being new to writing, was extraordinary at every turn. I could not have completed this project without her.

Morgan James Publishing has a unique approach to the publishing industry that perfectly met my needs for this book. Their team has been instrumental in turning a bunch of words on pages into a real book.

The overwhelming support and constructive feedback I received from proofreaders have dramatically improved the reading experience.

Without the time and effort of Rhiannon Gharibeh, Nancy Fishgold, Jonalyn Denlinger, and Justin Vaughn, *Fit Financial Approach* would be a far less comprehensible book.

Creatively, Tim Hughes has played a significant role in helping me mold an idea into content that will actually help people and reach as many as possible.

Jeff Motske, the founder and leader of Trilogy Financial, has provided the space for me to share my perspective on the world of finance and fitness. His guidance as an author, a financial planner, and a leader has been extremely influential in my work and life.

Finally, where would I be without my family? Kim, Dexter, Callen, and Greta provided support and love throughout this process that helped me persevere through times I wanted to walk away and stop writing. They have consistently been there for me, and I am a better writer, planner, leader, and man because of them.

PREFACE

I am a Certified Financial Planner (CFP®) and a Certified Personal Trainer (CPT); I am not a doctor, lawyer, CPA, or dietician.

My goal is to help you be fit physically and financially. Any of the health claims I make are from the fitness perspective. I did not go to medical school, and I don't claim to know everything in the health space. The studies I reference in the book may continue to improve over time, or the science may change. (That's the exciting part of science.) I will do my best to stick to the tried-and-true information in the fitness world; there's not much as most of the information out there is fluff. If you need health advice beyond the depth we reach for this book's purposes, please see a health professional. Before starting a fitness regimen, ask your doctor if you are physically able to do so. If you begin to feel pain or ill effects from your fitness regimen, please stop what you're doing and see a doctor. If you don't know what you're doing in the gym, have a professional help you. Personal trainers would be happy to show you around.

Any of the financial recommendations made in this book's pages are for educational purposes, not advice. For a good financial planner to give you unbiased, objective, and individualized advice in your best interest, they have to know your current financial situation intimately. I don't know your circumstances. Please use the information in this book to better your life. But, similarly to the doctor comment, if you need financial advice beyond the depth provided in the pages of this book, please seek the services of a financial planner.

BROKER-DEALER DISCLOSURE

Content in this material is for general information only and is not intended to provide specific advice or recommendations for any individual. All indices are unmanaged and may not be invested into directly. All investing involves risk including loss of principal. No strategy assures success or protects against loss. There is no guarantee that a diversified portfolio will enhance overall returns or outperform a non-diversified portfolio. Diversification does not protect against market risk. Bonds are subject to market and interest rate risk if sold prior to maturity. Bond values will decline as interest rates rise and bonds are subject to availability and change in price. Stock investing involves risk including loss of principal. Investing in mutual funds involves risk, including possible loss of principal. Alternative investments may not be suitable for all investors and should be considered as an investment for the risk capital portion of the investor's portfolio. The strategies employed in the management of alternative investments may accelerate the velocity of potential losses. An investment in Exchange Traded Funds (ETF), structured as a mutual fund or unit investment trust, involves the risk of losing money and should be considered as part of an overall program, not a complete investment program. An investment in ETFs involves additional risks such as not diversified, price volatility, competitive industry pressure, international political and economic developments, possible trading halts, and index tracking errors. Fixed and Variable annuities are suitable for long-term investing, such as retirement investing. Gains from tax-deferred investments are taxable as ordinary income upon withdrawal. Guarantees are based on the claims paying ability of the issuing company. Withdrawals made prior to age 59 ½ are subject to a 10% IRS penalty tax and surrender charges may apply. Variable annuities are subject to market risk and may lose value. Contributions to a traditional IRA may be tax deductible in the contribution year, with current income tax due at withdrawal. Withdrawals prior to age 59 ½ may result in a 10% IRS penalty tax in addition to current income tax. A Roth IRA offers tax deferral on any earnings in the account. Qualified withdrawals of earnings from the account are tax-free. Withdrawals of earnings prior to age 59 ½ or prior to the account being opened for five years, whichever is later, may result in a 10% IRS penalty tax. Limitations and restrictions may apply. Prior to investing in a 529 Plan investors should consider whether the investor's or designated beneficiary's home state offers any state tax or other state benefits such as financial aid, scholarship funds, and protection from creditors that are only available for investments in such state's qualified tuition program. Withdrawals used for qualified expenses are federally tax free. Tax treatment at the state level may vary. Please consult with your tax advisor before investing. This information is not intended to be a substitute for specific individualized tax advice. We suggest that you discuss your specific tax issues with a qualified tax advisor.

HEALTH & WEALTH

A Symbiotic Relationship

Imagine you're at the end of your entire working career. You were a captain of industry, leading men and women on the journey. You've saved money, and you can comfortably retire for the rest of your life. Phew. But…to acquire the financial rewards, you massacred your mental health. You stayed stressed for long periods of time to meet deadlines. You ruined relationships because you were never home for the key moments. You jeopardized your future quality of life by choosing to spend overtime in the office rather than taking care of yourself physically. You have all the money you'll need, but you lack the health—physical or mental—to enjoy it.

Now consider a different path. Imagine that while you did work hard, you also played hard. Your motto was, "Live for today and today only." Why deprive yourself of a luxury car just because the payment wouldn't allow you to save for your future? You exercised regularly to maintain your appearance, kept up with all your friends, and were always the life of the party. You've reached the end of your working years in good shape with great relationships. Congrats. But…you didn't save much, and you'll be forced to keep working until you die (so stay healthy) or make do with your social security income.

Which of these scenarios scares you more: the rich corpse or a healthy elder forever trapped inside an insufficient budget? They are equally the makings of a nightmare. If you have a ton of money without health, all your hard-earned money will likely be spent on doctors and hospitals. On the other side of the same issue, if you have your health without wealth, you can't travel like you wanted or spoil your grandkids. Don't end up fit and broke, or rich and broken. Neither situation will leave you happy. We all want—and dare I say, *need*—to have an appropriate fitness level in both health and wealth to live a full life while working and in retirement. Only a fraction of people earn enough money and have enough time to be rock stars in both arenas; the majority of us need to evaluate what's important to us now and in the future. Once you determine what is essential to make yourself happy in this life, you'll see your financial goals are mostly attainable, *and* you can be healthy enough to enjoy them.

Society as a whole, though, is getting worse in health and wealth. While we have more access to information than ever before, financial literacy is at all-time lows. Obesity already kills more people every year than terrorism, cancer, and war combined[1]. Stress is reaching an all-time high. Anxiety and depression are diagnosed at alarming rates.

The problem is health and wealth are symbiotically connected and work together in the downward spiral. One of the leading reasons for anxiety, depression, and stress is money.

When we have financial worries, we lose sleep, which is vital for our well-being. If we're not sleeping, we won't be as healthy, and we'll

---

1   Ritchie, H., & Roser, M. (2019, December). *Causes of Death*. Retrieved June 2020, from Our World in Data: http://ourworldindata.org/causes-of-death

have to visit the doctor or buy medicine more often, which then takes money away from our wealth. When we are stressed-out, we tend to make poor choices with our food and health habits. These habits feed off each other to make things worse. We're soon caught in a health-and-wealth death spiral, and fixing just one of the issues doesn't address the whole problem.

The good news is health and wealth work hand-in-hand on the upward spiral just as much as they work together on the downward one. Here are some statistics that demonstrate the positive correlation between health and wealth:

- ❏ "People can save up to $6,000 per year with healthier habits."[2]

- ❏ "An affluent 25-year-old will live six years longer than someone the same age who is less financially secure."[3]

- ❏ "People who take at least 10,000 steps a day are 21% more likely to maintain a budget."[4]

- ❏ "As of 2010, up to half of all premature deaths in the U.S. are due to preventable factors such as poor diet and lack of exercise."[5]

The overlap between health and wealth is astounding. Small steps in one area will affect the other. Suppose someone works to better their financial situation. In that case, they may start sleeping better, which typically leads to weight loss and a clearer mind, compounded with

---

2   Rutgers New Jersey Agricultural Experience, 2016
3   Virginia Commonwealth University Center on Society and Health, "Income and Health Initiative, 2015
4   Communicating on Wealth and Health, Deloitte Consulting LLP
5   "Measuring the Risks and Causes of Premature Death: Summary of Workshops," National Research Council (NRC) and Institute of Medicine, 2015

the fact this person carries far less stress on their shoulders day in and day out. Now, their health and wealth are working together toward a better future.

Throughout our lives, our wealth will affect our health and vice versa. We have to start making better decisions and building better habits to get our money and health into shape to improve our life experience and vitality.

In *The Power of Habit: Why We Do What We Do in Life and Business*, Charles Duhigg makes the case that self-control is like a muscle that can be trained and improved, and while you're working your self-control by not spending money on things you don't prioritize, you can also improve your health by using the same skill of self-control by eating at home rather than stopping for a fattening fast food dinner. Based on the research, focusing on fitness and finances could improve both areas by working the self-control muscle even more.

As a financial planner, I have to know many rules and laws. I need to understand the impact both mathematically and emotionally of the short and long-term decisions needed to help clients along their path. But after all of the math calculations and performance analyses, my actual job is helping clients build a plan and stick to it to reach their preferred future.

I'm not ripped; I don't have six-pack abs and huge biceps. I'm not the kind of rich that can buy a yacht or multiple homes. What I do have is experience helping people better their lives in both areas. I've seen thousands of clients attain new fitness levels in both health and wealth, enough to know being ultra-rich and ripped don't have anything to do with being fit and wealthy. Their success has shown me that the habits it takes for a client to achieve success in one area are the exact same habits needed to achieve success in the other. It makes sense that once you've decided to work on one of these areas of life, work on both. It won't take much more effort to better both aspects of your life. You just have to know how the rules apply and which habits to cultivate. Then take one step after the other on the spiral staircase of life that leads up to your goals.

This book aims to help stem the disastrous future we as a culture are heading towards if we stay on the current course. You can visualize what a better life could look like, no matter where or when you start. Inside these pages, you will find the information and motivation to make meaningful change, whether it's a massive turnaround from how you've managed habits until now or a slight modification to your positive practices already in place. The easy-to-follow guide will help you define your future, plan your path, and know what you need to do to improve *both* your fitness and finances.

Health, wealth, and happiness are the keys to a good life. Happiness is far easier to come by if you have both health and wealth. When you work in both areas, you will be amazed at the leaps and bounds you can make toward a better life, and achieving both health and wealth is not nearly as hard as you think.

The Fit Financial Formula

My life changed forever in health and wealth when I was 12 years old, and I woke up in a medevac helicopter, strapped to the patient table. Without some incredibly lucky timing and brilliant first responders, I would have bled out in the backseat of a car in rural Georgia. My parents had been driving my friend and me to dinner after bowling when a dually truck with a cement mixer hitched to the back skidded through a stop sign, t-boning my side of the car. The truck's grille took a chunk out of my forehead; metal scraps and glass shredded my cheek and chin. Dad suffered minor whiplash and jumped to our aid. Mom was shaken and pinned in by the damaged passenger's side door. My friend was screaming as he had glass in his eye, and I was unconscious and limp, held up by the seatbelt, with blood pouring out of my forehead. The surgeons later told me they had lost track of the number of sutures they sewed to stitch my face back together. It was a miracle I didn't have a broken skull.

Now, looking back as a father myself, I can't even imagine the horror my parents went through while waiting for the medical team to complete the reconstructive surgery that saved my life. Thankfully, I did survive, but I don't remember what life is like without scars on my face or the ongoing headaches caused by a pinched nerve in my shoulder. I used to have to pull over while driving because the migraines grew so painful, I had to vomit right then and there. I learned that regular chiropractor visits and maintaining a certain level of fitness kept the chronic headaches at bay. The ten years it took to figure out how not to get a headache every single day led me to become a personal trainer for a couple of years. I wanted to learn how to maintain my fitness the right way, and I loved helping others with their health decisions as well.

Once my parents overcame the initial scare of almost losing their son, the next round of worrying started: How would they pay all the medical bills? It must have been incredibly hard for my dad to go back to work as a pilot and leave his recovering son for days at a time. Two years later, we won a lawsuit for the accident and used some money from the settlement to pay the debts. I also took a portion of my proceeds and invested in a tech stock. It was 1999; technology stocks were going up, and I wanted to ride the wave. Ride the wave I did until the tech bubble burst in 2001. I basically lost the value of a car, but I learned a far more valuable lesson: I needed a plan. My dad took me to his financial advisor, and after listening and asking questions, I was hooked.

I connected the formula for health and wealth early on, and in the last 15 years, I have put the principles in this book to work in my own life and for my clients. The pathway to a healthy and wealthy life is more straightforward than you think. Maybe not always emotionally easy, but straightforward, yes. When you actively develop, hone, and implement the three pillars of progress—mindset, planning, and habits—to health and wealth, and you do that consistently over time, you will inevitably enhance your fitness and wealth. I'll explain the three pillars in later chapters, but the takeaway here is the simplicity of the Fit Financial formula:

[Mindset + Planning + Habits] + Time = Health & Wealth

Following this formula changes lives. I've seen it myself. If you are willing to live this formula, you can create a lifestyle that will remain long after you put this book down. By sticking with this formula over the years, you will reach your goals and far exceed what you thought was possible.

Mindset, planning, and habits are the three pillars of progress explored in this book. Each part of the formula is defined, and there are guided questions and exercises to help you determine what applying the Fit Financial Approach could look like when applied to your life now and in the future. The questions are available in a worksheet on my website, www.fitfinancialapproach.com, to follow along as well.

When it comes to eternal truths about human behavior, they are simple. Losing weight doesn't take a Ph.D. to figure out. I'll go into more detail later, but the basic rule is to eat less than you burn, or eat less and move more. Many diets and fad workout programs tell you it's more complicated than that. "All you have to do is buy my *(insert crazy, yet somewhat believable product here)*, and I can help you solve the riddle." There is no riddle.

We want to believe there's something more to being healthy than eat less, move more because if it is so simple, we ask ourselves, "why haven't I done it yet?" Typically, we haven't done it because we resist the commitment it takes. Plus, it seems like hard work to eat less. If you go to a restaurant today, they bring portion sizes large enough to feed at least three people twenty years ago. Being hungry doesn't feel good. Saying no to cookies, even though we know it's a healthy choice, isn't easy. I understand eating less feels like depriving yourself of something, but the math is clear. Move more, eat less.

Common Question: How much is 100 calories to eat or burn?

The FDA recommends a "normal person" eat 2,000 calories per day. This recommendation varies wildly between activity levels, body size, and the individuals' goals, but we'll stick with their recommendation for this exercise. I'd like to give some examples, so you can see what 100 calories really look like:

100 calories of carrots - 25 baby carrots
100 calories of potato chips - 8 chips
100 calories of almonds - 14 raw almonds
100 calories of eggs - slightly less than 1 1/2 eggs
100 calories of gummy bears - 11 bears!
100 calories of sandwich cookies - 2 cookies

This is not to say each of the examples above are equal. Obviously, some have more nutritional value than others, but you get the idea. Two thousand calories don't amount to much in many of today's food choices.

I thoroughly enjoy a Chick-fil-A chicken sandwich meal with medium waffle fries and a medium lemonade. Based on information from the Chick-fil-A website, that meal alone consists of 1,020 calories. After that meal, there isn't much room to eat within your recommended daily calories. And, how often have you taken up the kid behind the counter on the 50-cent upgrade to the large?

Now you've eaten 1200 calories, or 60% of the FDA's recommendation, in one meal.

The most challenging part of eating less is only difficult for a little while. Two reasons for that: One, once you have measured your food and tracked your calories for a couple of weeks, you get a good feel for what 100 calories look like. Two, once you have built a habit, you don't have to think so much, and doing becomes second nature. Let's say you've developed a habit of waking up at 5:30 a.m. to work out before the kids are up; you will feel out of sync with your natural rhythm when you *don't* wake up and workout. That's when you know you're living a healthy lifestyle. That's also when you start annoying your coworkers because you complain you haven't been <u>able</u> to work out all week. They won't get it, and you'll smile…then hand them a copy of this book. This *will* happen to you if you start following the Fit Financial formula. (Please contact me through www.fitfinancialapproach.com to let me know when it happens to you. I love to hear these things.)

The same rule of simplicity applies to finances. It is not easy to become wealthy, but it is simple. You can follow some basic rules to get there, but they won't feel good at first. For instance, all you have to do to pay down debt and save money is spend less than you make. Guess what? It's the same rule as eat less, move more. The math is simple: calculate where your money is going, where it's coming from, and the difference between the two to get started. Yet, money is emotional for people. During the great recession of 2008, a local news channel interviewed me to discuss the market. I told the newscasters and the audience watching that the stock market wasn't just down. It was on sale. "Think of it as the Black Friday sales in retail stores," I said.

Mathematically, I was correct, but no one wanted to hear it. While the masses lashed out at me through social media, my clients stayed the course with their plans. In the short term, they weren't always happy with their return on investment, but they were better off in the long run. The heated reactions of the general public taught me the math was not always the issue. Financial planning is partially about making sure the numbers line up, but the most critical aspect is the emotional decision-making.

Common Question: How much will $100 a month be in 20 years?

Today, you can buy $100 worth of groceries with a $100 bill. Makes sense, right? In 20 years—given an assumed 2% rate of inflation—you will be able to buy approximately $67 worth of groceries in today's dollars for today's $100. If inflation is 3.6%, you'd only get $50 worth of today's groceries in 20 years with the same $100 bill.

$100 today, 20 years later at 2% inflation = $67
$100 today, 20 years later at 3.6% inflation = $50

Think of a home you may have purchased in the past. My dad bought our family home in Peachtree City, GA, in December 1983 for $99,000. Today, while writing this in October 2018, the almost exact same home—same boards in much the same place with some different colors and updated appliances—is worth an estimated $345,000. That's an average growth rate of 3.63%. For the most part, real estate increases at the rate of inflation over long periods. If this rate continues for another 20 years, the same house will be worth $704,000.

You can buy less with the same amount of money over time. This is why it is imperative to start early with your savings and take some risk, so you can at least keep up with but hopefully beat inflation over long periods of time.

The Fit Financial formula works because rather than focusing on one area, we focus on both health and wealth at the same time. It doesn't just tackle the numbers. It includes working with your natural emotional needs, forming supportive habits, and shifting your mindset for a successful life.

You can learn to tackle the emotional blocks and use these tools to implement the simple formula for a full life of being both fit and wealthy, but the hard part is in the squishy gray thing between your ears: your brain. You must decide to change. You have to decide you want to be both healthy and wealthy and are willing to take simple steps over a long time. You have to believe no silver bullet will solve all your problems in a matter of days or weeks. I will teach you the simple, effective way to live a healthier, more prosperous life, but it is up to you to incorporate these life lessons into your day-to-day activities and make the change. To get started, we need to cut through the noise and get to the fact of the matter.

Cutting Through the Misinformation

Before we set up financial and health goals and make choices about how to get you down the path to those goals, we have to cut through the misinformation out there. Unfortunately, there's a lot of it. If you do an online search for "fitness tips," there are over 1.4 billion results. The search also gives you several other options like "fitness tips for beginners" and "fitness tips for women." This is the problem, and the same happens when you ask for "financial planning." There are many opinions out there, and only some of them are based on actual facts. Most of these articles and websites base their statements around pseudo-science. I can't get to all of it, but let's cover some of the most visible nonsense found in both industries.

Check Expectations Against Reality

The problem with both health and wealth is societal expectations and reality don't match. I grew up watching shows like "Dream Car Garage" and "Cribs," where people showcased their outrageously expensive and typically unnecessary lifestyles. Watching shows like this leads people to think, "I could have that life someday." I'm sorry to be the bearer of bad news: You probably won't. Maybe you can if you are wildly talented *and* fortunate with opportunities at the right times in your life. Then once you have talent and luck, you'll have to work your butt off, too. The number of people who actually meet the super-rich level is so low you're probably better off playing the lottery. (Please don't.) Either way, the odds are not good.

For health, models with six-pack abs and chiseled features are plastered all over magazines and TV. They all pretend to eat pizza and burgers while smoking cigarettes and watching Netflix; I promise you this is not the case. Achieving a body like those fitness freaks happen one of two ways. Either they work like crazy over a long period, eat perfectly for months, and in the last two weeks basically starve and dehydrate themselves to capture the "cut" look. This fitness regimen and the look are not sustainable for longer than the camera is rolling. Today's more common option in the fitness modeling world is the "cut" phase happens after the camera shuts off, and some whiz with Photoshop shaves the love handles and adds shadows to the model's abs.

In either case, the world of fitness modeling portrays a reality that does not exist, and the false advertising drives me nuts. Yes, you can get in great shape if you eat right and exercise, but don't expect to reach unrealistic levels in either fitness or wealth. If you work your butt off, eat correctly, and maintain that discipline over a long time while having great genes, you could get there. But, in most cases, you can't, and shooting for unrealistic, unfounded goals leads to discouragement, paralysis, and a "why bother?" complacency. I'd prefer to have you strive for a healthy and wealthy life you can live into, given your current reality. I'm guessing you are a real person. Maybe your genes aren't perfect, and you hold the fat on your stomach above your abdominal muscles instead of those fitness models lucky enough to hold the fat cells underneath their abs. Maybe your work, family life, social life, or other constraints on your time won't allow you to spend hours focusing on your body through meal preparation and time in the gym. And maybe you're not in a place in life or have the resources or connections to start the next company to go public and make a bajillion dollars. If your life is like most of us, the Fit Financial Approach is made for you. It is designed to be applied to a *real* life: your life.

Reality is more fun anyway. Think, for a moment, about what you are really trying to accomplish. For example, do you want six-pack abs because you think it will impress your wife? It won't impress her as much as playing with your kids on a Sunday afternoon. Are you trying to buy a house for your mom, so you can tell your friends how rich you are? Seriously, your friends may not know how much money you have in your 401k but being financially independent in a reasonable amount of time will make them jealous, I promise. And, for the record, I don't recommend *creating jealousy* as a healthy goal for your finances or fitness. We will get to goal setting, but the first step on a path to attainable financial wellness is a gut check: what current lifestyle does it take—financially and health-wise—to achieve the exact things you want now and in the future? Let's start here:

What I really want to get out of life is...

_____

_____

_____

_____

For me, I want to stay healthy enough to play with my kids as long as they want to play with me. I know one day I won't be cool enough for them, but I will be there, running alongside them for as long as I am cool in their eyes. In finances, I just want to have enough money set aside to protect my family from an emergency, feel comfortable in our lifestyle, and travel from time to time. I love what I do, so I don't intend to stop working any time soon.

My answer to what I really want out of life is to make a difference for others. Making a difference for others does not require me to be ripped or have millions of dollars in the bank; I can motivate and inspire you just by practicing what I preach and struggling the same way you do every day. I want to help people attain their fitness and financial goals, so they can focus on the things that matter to them. If all of us focused a little more on what we care about, the world would be a far better place. When I get out of my own head about how I look or feel and focus on helping others, more people get my attention. I'm just one person but think of the difference if thousands of people focused on their valued priorities. Once someone starts seeing the benefits of fitness in health and wealth, their progress has crossover effects on friends and family. Their fit lifestyle inspires those they love to make changes; I have seen entire extended families quit smoking within the same year, falling like dominoes. The example they set shows their loved ones it is possible to withstand the urge to step outside for a cigarette, and soon the others think, "I could quit, too."

Effects are generative, and I know the person I help will motivate and inspire several more. If I can inspire you to stop comparing your life to "reality" television, set realistic health and wealth goals, and go do what is paramount to you, we can change the world together—no big deal.

Instant Gratification Kills Dreams

Another problem in both the health and wealth arenas is the instant gratification culture we live in. The Veruca Salt mentality of "I want it, and I want it now" is totally unrealistic. Nothing in this world worthwhile to achieve comes easily or quickly. It will take time to be wealthy. It will take time to be fit. That's okay. The end of the road in this journey is not a destination; you will never get to a point and say to yourself, "Okay, I made it. Now I can blow a bunch of money and eat cheeseburgers every day," because once you reach the goals you have today, you'll set new goals for tomorrow. I've seen it time and again. At the very least, you'll want to maintain the level of health and wealth you've achieved today, and maintenance takes staying the course of the life you've built. People don't get rich because they blow their hard-earned money on whatever tickles their fancy. They get rich because they prioritize wealth over instant gratification. Once they reach their financial goals, they can't waste money on the things they don't care about all of a sudden, or they won't stay wealthy forever.

If all you're working toward is a destination so you can go back to the habits that made you unhappy in the first place, you will never be happy as you'll eventually end up right where you are now. People who start the Fit Financial journey set goals, crush them, and repeat. They are always striving for the next thing, and the process itself is what makes them happy with their fitness in health and wealth.

Immediate gratification is a good way to kill any long-term goal. There is one universal truth acting against immediate gratification: you cannot buy the life you want. You can buy all the toys you want, but if you're miserable in general, you will continue to be miserable after you get off the wave runner. So, get off the instant gratification ride altogether. You'll know when you're on the path to financial and physical success because you'll be proud of the journey. You'll be enjoying the ride, not trying to get to your destination as quickly as you can.

Deprivation is Hard and Unnecessary

We fall for the "Cribs" and "I want it now" culture because the human condition doesn't like to perceive it's being deprived of anything. I don't fault anyone for this. It's part of our makeup, our DNA; you can't avoid feeling like this. Unfortunately, the "mad men" (and women) at marketing firms all around the world know this too. They know this red button, and they press it all the time. Watch any pharmaceutical ad on TV: "Do you feel like life isn't going your way? Do you feel like you could be happier? Would you be more productive if you felt happier?" Of course you do, and of course you would. Their solution is to go to your doctor and buy this-or-that drug.

In a more subtle style of commercial ad, they show you a lifestyle no one has. Then they promise you can also drive on the Pacific Coastal Highway in California without any traffic during a romantic sunset on a perfect fall day. You, too, can be dressed in the perfectly pressed pair of khakis with your cashmere sweater draped over your shoulder like you have no cares in the world. Your perfect kids will be in the back seat reading their books with smiles on their faces, and your wife will realize how perfect your life is while she reaches over to play with the hair at the top of your neck. Now you've bought in; of course, you want that life.

Then they hit you with the sales pitch. All you have to do is buy the car that guy is driving, and you can have the same experience. No—again, the bearer of bad news—you probably won't. You'd be sitting in dead-stopped traffic staring at the smog in Los Angeles. Your kids will be going nuts in the back seat with their snack somehow stuck to the roof of the car, and your wife will be checking social media to see how great everyone else's life is right now. All you got out of the deal was a sweet car and a huge car payment.

Unfortunately, every ad you see manipulates you like this. They are trying to make you feel left out by selling you a life you can't buy, no matter how much money you have. Once they have you dreaming of the dream, you feel deprived of the life the perfect family has in their perfect car. In the real world, the film crew blocked the road and created traffic detours for the rest of the Los Angeles residents on that perfect fall day, so they didn't even get to enjoy the setting.

Then you have fad diets and get-rich-quick schemes on top of it. These ads are working against reality and creating scenarios where people are depriving themselves all the time, and the advertisers are masters at subconsciously getting in front of you. Someone is on TV or the radio every minute of every day to tell you they got rich or lost a ton of weight doing something really easy, and you can do it too. All you have to do is buy their book that explains how they did it, so you can go out and follow in their footsteps. Most of the time, the person selling the fad diet/workout scheme did not get into great shape doing what they are telling you to do, and the person who gets rich quick in this scenario is not you; it's the guy or gal selling the books, DVDs, classes, and so on who make money. Don't fall for any of this. It won't do any good at best, and at worst, these diets and schemes can do real damage. The get-rich-quick schemes can lead someone to take on more risk than is suitable. For instance, buying a house with zero percent down, fixing it up, and flipping it when you don't have a safety net of cash or experience in the business is risky. The market could turn. You could be unable to make the mortgage payment when something changes at work and lose the investment. With fad diets, people typically have to give something up like carbohydrates, meat, alcohol, or whatever else the diet says to avoid. When we deprive ourselves of something we like, the likelihood we will binge when the fad diet is done goes through the roof. This is why people typically gain the weight back after one of these diets.

The dirty little secret the ad companies and salespeople don't want you to know is living the life you want isn't as hard as they want you to think. It takes longer, yes, but it isn't complicated. Getting healthy and wealthy is a lifelong journey that can actually be fun and not feel like deprivation at all. While you cannot get wealthy buying every option of the fanciest cars or get healthy eating ice cream and cookies every day, the good news is you can still have the options you care about, and you don't have to give up ice cream and cookies completely. When you consume the things you enjoy less frequently, you will enjoy them even more.

If you told me in college that eating less pizza would be good for me, I would have called bull. I love pizza, and not the gourmet, somewhat healthy kind of pizza. I like the greasy, heavy kind of pizza. I'm not depriving myself of pizza, but I eat it only once a month or so. That's okay. I also drink beer. We have all kinds of unhealthy treats to eat all over the house, and I eat them in moderation. I eat gummies and have more than once given myself a stomachache from eating too many in one sitting. Who decided 5lbs of Red Vines in one container was a good idea? I also spend more on technology than I need to, and I'm frivolous with spending when it comes to going out to eat. We go out to eat so rarely these days with little kids at home that I am willing to spend a few extra dollars on a good bottle of wine and a great meal. I'm a disciplined and goal-oriented person, but I am far from perfect. I would argue that depriving yourself to be perfect is counterproductive.

If what you're really looking for in health and wealth is realistic, you won't need to make such hard lifestyle changes you'll never stick to. You can maintain a healthy lifestyle and set aside money for your top goals at the same time. You don't have to eat wheatgrass and save 50% of your income to get there. I hate wheatgrass. You don't have to be perfect when you're realistic about what you want and why. I'm probably not going to have six-pack abs ever again. I also don't need to have a chiseled physique to have the life I want to live. I just need to be in shape enough to feel physically and mentally sound and able to play with my kids. The same goes for spending. I am funding most of my goals to an appropriate level. I don't really need to worry about expenses unless I'm stealing from those goals to do something today.

We can spend extra money at times for things we want today now that we have earned the ability to do so. It wasn't always that way, but we have worked to get there over time.

Once you have realistic expectations for your life, your indulgences aren't awful mistakes but a nice reward every so often for sticking to the right habits. The point is to move toward your goals, or what is important to you, one step at a time. There will be times in your life when it's easier to take those steps and times when it isn't easy at all. You don't have to be perfect all the time forever, but you may have to be more perfect at times in your life, so you can reach the flexibility you're looking for later.

Owning Stuff isn't Wealth

"He who is not contented with what he has, would not be contented with what he would like to have." ~ Socrates

Wealth means something different for every person, and financial goals come in all shapes and sizes. I have clients who tell me their version of wealth is the security of knowing they will be okay in the future and not run out of money. They don't need fancy cars, big houses, or other material things reality television tells all of us we "should" want. They just want to be comfortable in their simple life. Other clients have big dreams of traveling the world, golfing on as many PGA rated courses as possible, or playing their fiddle in the fiddle club while visiting the Shetland Islands. Some of my clients would like to buy *stuff* as part of their future financial goals, but there is typically a sentimental attachment to it, like my client who wants to buy a car similar to the one her father built for her when she was sixteen. Owning physical objects is an entirely appropriate goal, so long as your reason for owning them drives you to go after what you want.

Time and time again, unhappy clients with a goal to own something—without a driving attachment—acquire it and are still unhappy.

One particular client couldn't understand why. He said to me, "I've been working for years to buy a BMW. Now that I have one, I realize it's just a car, and it doesn't have enough cup holders." His true goal was a lifestyle he thought owning a BMW would provide. Whatever your BMW may be, it won't buy you a lifestyle. You have to create that life one step at a time. It takes more than just money and *stuff* to get the life you want. It takes knowing the life you want and where finances fit inside that life. Money is just a means to an end. We will work to determine what that money is for and how to build the wealth to get there.

The Market Has Little to Do with Long-Term Financial Success

Whenever I tell someone I'm a financial planner, they usually try their best to walk away. Understandable, really. Most people assume I'm going to go one of two ways: either try to sell them a product right there on the spot (no one does this) or start spouting information about the market, boring everyone to tears. Of course, I'm not going to do either of these. One, I only want to help people who are ready to make better decisions with their money over time. Two, I don't try to guess what the market is going to do and don't feel comfortable telling anyone what to do on a short-term basis. I don't need to know what's happening at any given time, and neither do you. What the market did over the last day, week, month, or more has little to do with your financial success over the course of a lifetime.

The market typically goes up over a long period of time. That doesn't mean it will always go up, and in those decades where the market does go up, there are usually several short-term pull-backs within the period. Do not let these short-term perspectives throw you off your game. You're in this for the long haul. The best thing you can do with your long-term investments is to look at the quarterly statements to verify nothing has drastically changed and ignore the news. The news is not trying to give you information; they are trying to sell ads. When the market is going down, that's all you'll hear about. When it's up the same percentage, you're lucky even to catch it scrolling across the bottom of the screen. Down days sell ads because people freak out and keep watching. Don't freak out.

> Common Misconception: Women can get super bulky
>
> I know many women have reservations about engaging in resistance training because they don't want to look like those body-building women who could crush my head like a grape. Don't worry. While a strong woman is a beautiful look, strong does not equate to "big" or "bulky." The vast majority of women do not have the testosterone levels to support such large muscles in their bodies. Don't get me wrong, you can become super strong, but the huge sizes won't come without medicinal help from the outside. Those enormous bodybuilders you see in magazines take the types of supplements that alter body chemistry and add testosterone.
>
> If you believe you are a genetic anomaly who can put on some bulk without supplementing your hormones, stick to lower weights with more repetitions, just to be sure.

What impacts your financial plan most is making more good decisions than bad ones over the long haul. If you make a mistake, it's okay. Keep moving forward. Did I say you have to be perfect? No. Just make more good decisions than bad decisions over time. That's it. Few people invest in a company like Amazon when it's a cute, infant book sales website and sell when the company becomes so large it runs long-standing retailers out of business. There's just no way to know which company is going to hit it big. At the time Amazon started, other website companies delivered groceries, medications, dog treats, or other consumer goods to your door. Many of those companies didn't survive the tech bubble burst, and their investors were left with nothing. There are more stories of investors left holding the bag than there are of a company's investors getting ludicrously wealthy. You don't hear the bag-holding stories because no one working out at the gym or talking to their brother-in-law brags about a bad investment.

My point is to let the neurosis go and get off the emotional roller-coaster of keeping up with the financial market news; the market will do what the market does. Control what you can control, which is your habits and discipline over time. Use the tried-and-true methods covered in this book like dollar-cost averaging and diversification over a long time to secure your financial future. Keep moving forward, even if you have to cut contributions or change your plan due to a change in circumstances. Just keep putting one foot in front of the other on the path to financial fitness.

Having Abs is Not Health

Health is not having six-pack abs or running marathons, no matter what the fitness magazines try to tell you. Living a healthy lifestyle means giving yourself the best chance to physically perform at the level you need at any given time now or in the future. If you live in an area with wild tigers you may need to outrun at some point, you better be fit enough to do so. If like me, you live in a reasonably safe neighborhood (especially from tigers), and you just want to be able to play with your three kids who seem to have boundless energy, you still need to be in good shape, but not quite tiger-avoidance shape.

I know my kids will soon be able to outrun me, but that doesn't mean I won't put up a fight. I still remember the day I beat my dad in wrestling. The day you beat your parents at something is a rite of passage in a kid's life. I plan to make that day as far away as possible for my kids. I also want to ensure I will be able to bend down, get on the floor, and play with my grandkids when they're visiting someday in the future. Think about that: I am talking about being healthy and active for at least 30-40 years just to keep up with my kids and grandkids. I'd also like to be able to take my family all over the world one day; there's a lot of walking involved with traveling. I want to be able to see all of Paris when we go, not just half of it because I'm tired and need to take frequent breaks. Finally, I want to live a long time, so I can see my kids grow up and become additive members of society who strive for their goals, whatever they may be.

Does any of the above require extreme flexibility or the ability to ride a bike over a mountain pass? No, of course not. Sometimes I think I want those things, but it's not realistic to have them forever. I may train for a marathon one day since I am awful at running and may want to prove to myself I could do it. I may develop toned abs at any given time through my workouts and efforts, but I know they are not the goal. They are the byproduct of my goals mentioned above. You can have these short-term goals for your health, but you must have a higher purpose to remain healthy if you want to maintain a desired lifestyle your whole life. I love running obstacle course races like the Tough Mudder and Spartan races, but racing is not my end game. I train harder when I have a race coming up, but they are not why I want to keep moving. My lifestyle in the future is the reason I train.

What does health mean to you? Why do you want to keep moving? Who are you trying to stay alive for? If there's a short-term goal in there, what mountains do you want to climb, finish lines do you want to cross, or oceans do you want to swim?

_____

_____

Common Misconception: Sit-ups will give you abs

Your core muscles do more for your body besides draw lusting or jealous stares at the beach. Your core connects your upper body with your lower body. Your core muscles help you bend, walk upright, twist, lift objects, and breathe. So yes, they are crucial to the routine, daily functioning of a human being. While having a strong core will make you better equipped to handle the functions above and then some, you cannot train your abs with only one exercise. If you do sit-ups all day, you will be better at one thing: sitting up. Oh, and you won't start seeing ripped abs just from being able to sit up better; that takes a concerted effort of muscle development and clean eating.

Having a stronger core can help with lower back pain. A strong core is also one of the foundations of a well-rounded level of fitness. If you want to lift more, work your core. If you want to sit with better posture, work your core. Want to run farther with less fatigue? Work your core. You see where we're heading. Work your core.

Fortunately, sit-ups will help you develop the abdominal muscles in your core. Unfortunately, for those looking for the beach-ready six-pack, as the muscles get bigger, they will look bigger, not necessarily more defined. If you have a layer (or more) of fat on top of your abdominal muscles, as the muscles get bigger, they will push the fat out farther. You can imagine what that does for self-esteem. You've been doing all these sit-ups, and all you've accomplished is looking fatter. What the hell?!? I have heard this story many times before, and there are really only two things you have to do to get that washboard look.

1. You have to work your entire core. You will need exercises like planks, twists, boats, leg lifts, spiders, back flexes, windshield wipers, and yes, sit-ups and crunches.

2. You will need to eat right. I know... This is the last thing you wanted to hear.

Like it or not, **abs are made in the kitchen, not the gym**. To see those shredded, washboard abs, you have to get the fat off the top of them. It takes discipline and attention if you want to get down to low body fat percentages, but it will get easier as you create the right habits like everything else. Teach your body to crave healthy foods instead of sugar, fat, and salt. If you value abs, stop eating crap and start burning calories. It will take time, but you'll get there eventually.

The Gym Has Little to do With Your Long-Term Health Success

Hitting the gym has something to do with being healthy, but it's not the be-all and end-all. You don't have to feel bad when you miss a day. You won't get into the shape you want to be in by lifting weights, running on a treadmill, or doing pushups alone. There is no special sauce at the gym to make you a healthy person. In my time as a trainer at a busy gym in Denver, many people came every single day and were not any healthier after months of working out than they were when they started. Maybe their workouts kept them from declining into a worse position, but they were not healthier. We've all seen these people in the locker rooms. After 30 minutes on the stair stepper, they get off only to grab a 300-calorie protein bar and wash it down with 250 calories of a sugary sports drink. Way to ruin the work you just did.

The same habitual decisions that make you wealthy will make you healthy: making more good decisions than bad ones over a long period of time. Are you going to be fat for the rest of your life because you just ate a 1lb cheeseburger with a side of fries? I will tell you from experience, no, you won't. Will you be fat the rest of your life if you eat 2,000 calories in a single sitting, four days a week, for years? Yeah, probably.

Don't do that. You can still make decisions not in line with your goals every so often, but the trick is to be mindful of the number of those decisions, so you can make more goal-aligned decisions to make up the difference over time. If you keep the unhealthy things you love in your diet, but you only eat them in moderation from time to time and balance them out with some good decisions, you won't be on a fad diet anymore.

The same is true with your trips to the gym or whatever you do to stay fit. All you have to do is stay active more often than not. You may not love the stair stepper or the treadmill, but I have met many people who hated cardio equipment but loved hiking or walking in the woods. Just remain active. And it's far easier to stay active if you're doing something you enjoy. If you are more active than not over a long period of time, you don't have to feel ashamed of the entire day you spend every so often on the couch binge-watching a show. It's okay… You can go for a walk, hike, run, bike ride, swim, yoga class, or whatever it is you love to do tomorrow. You'll be living a healthy lifestyle, and that's what is important.

You Don't Have to Set Goals to Start

If setting goals scares you because you haven't made decisions on where you want your life to go just yet, don't worry. You do not have to have goals. When asked about their goals, many young people will say, "Um, I guess I want to buy a house." When someone tells me a goal like this, I'll ask several questions. What research have you done? What neighborhood would you like to live in? How much are the average homes in the area? Do you want a two-story home? How about a basement? You get the idea. Typically, if the goal isn't an actual priority for the client, they won't answer any of these questions.

I don't want you to have goals just to have them. A perfectly acceptable goal is, "I don't know what the money is for just yet, but I know I will need it eventually." Don't add goals to your goal sheet just because you think someone else in a similar situation should have that goal. You'll never make the choices it takes along the way to reach a goal you don't care about. I've seen clients in both health and wealth who have one goal in their head as it's the logical thing to want and another goal in their heart as it's the future they authentically desire. The client typically ends up with competing goals like "I want to lose weight" and "I want to gain muscle and strength." Those two objectives are competing for most people as you have to add mass to gain muscle, and mass adds weight. Give yourself permission to want what you want or to not know what you want. Both of these options are acceptable, and you can still take steps toward your eventual health and wealth journey without concrete targets.

Once again, advertising wants you to think you have desires you don't actually have. If you find yourself thinking the luxury watch will change how you experience life and how people see you, stop. Immediately. However, if you admire the attention to detail and craftsmanship that a fine timepiece represents, then by all means. That's a great goal to strive for because you want it for you instead of wanting a life you don't currently have. Remember, you can't buy the life you crave; you have to work for it and live into it.

Often, people take the initial steps without goals, and soon after that, their goals become clear. They start working out and find out they really like riding a road bike. Now their goal is to develop strength in their legs to gain power on the inclines during their rides. I've seen people save some money in their "house fund" only to realize they love to travel and would rather own an apartment where they can turn off the water heater and head out the door for weeks at a time. It's incredible how decisions can lead to goals almost as well as goals can lead to decisions.

You Are Not Your Six Pack or Your Bank Account

During this process of finding what is important to you and taking steps to get there, you may start seeing some real results in your body, mind, and net worth. If I'm doing my job appropriately to motivate and educate you, and you're doing your job of getting out there and implementing some of this education, we will see results.

In my experience as an out-of-shape adolescent, my expectations were not met when I did actually reach my goals. I joined the wrestling team in my high school because those guys were ripped, and I wanted to get there, too. After grueling workouts wearing sweat bags to drop weight, I was in pretty good shape. What I *thought* was going to happen was I would be walking around all the time thinking about how good of shape I was in. Of course, I now know that only a sociopath could think about themselves like that all the time. I still had the same teenage angst I had before being in shape. I still had the same issues, the same thoughts, the same everything; I was just in shape. It was only through self-reflection I realized I am not my six-pack. My looks do not define me. We are all the same underneath, and health is just a tool to reach other life goals.

Money is the same way. Once you get off of the merry-go-round of month-to-month living, you start saving some money. Things get a bit easier, you're less stressed, and you save more money. You keep going until you have a net worth you can be proud of. Guess what? No one cares. No one will come up and say, "Hey, I noticed you're doing well. Congratulations," other than maybe your parents and your financial planner. Your money is a means to an end. The end may be the lower stress, more comfortable life. It could be you want to be retired at 40. Whatever it is, the money is not the end goal. You are not your bank account balance. Money is a tool to reach other life goals.

If money and health are simply tools, then the question becomes, what can your tools help you build?

The hardest part of this process is knowing yourself. It's not easy to know what you want to create, what you want out of life. There are distractions and shiny objects along the way that direct our attention from what is important to us. One distraction is watching reality television and the ironically unrealistic lives the stars live while the television networks try to sell you on why you want that life. That life doesn't really exist. It's just a production, filmed, edited, and touched-up to show you exactly what they want you to see. You may see a friend retired at 35 after selling his app that makes uncomfortable noises at random times (or whatever your friend's app does). He wonders every day if those awful noises are the extent of his value to humanity. He may not articulate those words in just that way, especially not to you, but I promise he's contemplating his value in the quiet times alone. We all question our value and our worth at times.

Take the next steps in this book seriously, so you can better know yourself and what you, in your heart, care about. This book will help you begin to discover what you want. If you need someone else to support you in this, grab a trusted friend and take them to coffee once a week until you feel confident and clear in your path. I have had many long, in-depth conversations about my priorities in life with good friends over coffee. Having a good friend listen and give their perspective helps immensely. Others can sit and write alone to understand themselves better. Whatever it is you need to do, do it. Put the unnecessary noise where it belongs and think about what you value in yourself and your life.

If you can take the time and put in the effort to go through this process, the rest of this book—the mindset, education, and motivation to change your life—will become exponentially easier.

Start by listing the five things you want right now in the table below. Make that list in the spaces below before reading on to the next paragraph.

Now, on the line next to those five things, write "Should" if it's a goal you think you *should* have but don't really want. Write "You" if it's a thing you want for someone else. Write "Me" if it's your authentic wish. Do this before moving to the next stage.

Okay, next to the items categorized as "me," write why you want them.

| List 5 things you want right now | Should, You, Me | Why? |

1. _____

2. _____

3. _____

4. _____

5. _____

We dive deeper into self-reflection in the Pillars of Progress section.

PILLARS OF PROGRESS

Mindset

If you're set on losing some weight for a specific event like a wedding or graduation, that is a great short-term goal, but your vision must be much further out when thinking about your health. If you're saving for a house or have a question about your retirement funds, your question will likely be answered within these pages, but you will not become wealthy unless you're looking to the horizon. You don't need to love exercise and saving. Most people don't, but you need an open mind to *become* someone who loves exercise, eating right, spending on your priorities, and seeing progress on your savings.

The first pillar of progress and the initial piece of the Fit Financial formula is your mindset. You have a lifetime ahead of you to make positive decisions (with a few not so positive ones mixed in from time to time). The mindset must have progress as the reward in order to change your future, not revert back to your old ways and gain the weight, or the debt, back again. You don't need that mindset today, but you need to be open to it. Are you open to changing your perspective?

Start by creating a mindset of positivity around health and wealth. *Eat good food because you love yourself,* not because you hate the way you look. This point is critical, so I will reiterate: do the work to improve your health and wealth because you love yourself and those close to you, not because you hate a piece of who you are. This distinction is significant. If you love yourself and eat well, your looks will change, but changing how you look best comes as an effect of a fundamental, positive mindset and lifestyle.

Focus on the Emotional 'Why'

As I've mentioned, decisions are not just logical; they are also emotional. Logic and emotion both have merit and are considered in your decision-making process. It's human nature to make a decision emotionally and afterward use logic to confirm that decision. This is where buyer's remorse comes from: you bought something because it was shiny and you liked it, but when logically reflecting on the purchase later, realized you didn't need or value the item nearly as much as in the moment you bought it. If you decide with an emotional why, you will value your decision, and you're more likely to stick with something that doesn't come naturally to you.

Prioritizing your health and wealth needs to be emotional. Have a why other than "society tells me I need to be muscular and rich." What are you doing this for? If you can't think of an emotional reason to remain healthy or save for your future, you'll never do the work it takes. Your reasons can and will change throughout your life, but it's crucial to start with a real reason that generates a strong positive emotional response when you think about it. The reasons for building and maintaining health and wealth I hear most often are family, confidence in job and life, preparation for the next financial crisis (Zombie apocalypse. No kidding, he was serious.), ending up in a better situation than my parents.

The most influential resources in your life are time and money, and you already know now that fitness in both will lead to more of both resources. What are the reasons you want more time and more money? Believe me. You have a reason. You just need to have the self-awareness to know what it is and keep it in the front of your mind when things get hard. Your why will keep you going.

Unfortunately, you can't just sit in your living room chair, close your eyes, and think about your why. Make decisions and take action to learn real lessons about yourself. Many friends from my past tried to, as they would say, "find themselves." They traveled the world with money they didn't have to try and discover what their life *should* be about. I'm pretty sure they came back with more debt than before and were still confused about who they were. I've found that we learn what we value by what we won't allow, by what we are willing to stand for when push comes to shove. In my own experience, I had grandiose ideas of what I would stand for in my life when I was sitting on the couch thinking without any real-world experience. When I went out in the world and had to actually do something about those thoughts, I found, while it was a great idea to stand for something, you have to sacrifice something else. You may have to stand up for yourself or someone else and sacrifice your job, a relationship, or some other aspect of your life for a value that holds more weight. If you're willing to give up an important aspect of your life for a value, that's what you stand for. Treat others with respect, even if you don't share the same beliefs or values. I've walked away from long-standing friendships because of bigotry and disrespect that I thought unnecessary and wrong. When you really value something in your life, as soon as that value is triggered, you feel it in your gut, and you can't help but do something about it. Once you know your own values, it can help you find your emotional reason to keep going when the going gets tough.

When I served as the Managing VP for the Denver office of Trilogy, I valued authenticity. When a representative asked me how they could make prospective clients think they are trustworthy, be a good planner, or do any other positive thing that would help their career, my answer was always the same. *Be* whatever you want people to think you are; that will speak louder than anything you could say. Don't try to look like you are a certain way, BE IT. Every time I have this conversation, I get highly animated; I can feel it in my gut, and my intensity has even scared some. After experiencing these physical reactions a few times, I realized authenticity is imperative to me. I even carry around a pen with the phrase "Esse Quam Videri"— Latin for "to be rather than to appear"— scribed on the side. Authenticity matters.

Knowing your why will keep you motivated through thick and thin. It's not imperative you know your why to take the first step, but pay attention, and your steps will help you define the why. Simon Sinek has a great book on this point called *Start with Why* if you'd like to dive deeper. To find your values, you'll need to go out into the world, experience life, and pay attention. For now, take notice when you are animated and feel a tingle in your stomach. Evaluate what set you into motion. Let's take some time for self-analysis to determine what is important to you.

I would imagine health and wealth fit in with your values; otherwise, you wouldn't have read this far into the book. Take a few minutes to answer the following questions to determine what those values could be and why you want to stay fit in health and finance.

Having your specific "why" will help you stay on the path when it becomes challenging and push you a little harder when you want to slack off

When in the past have you felt genuine excitement and your stomach tingled? When have you taken a stand for something, even when you had to sacrifice to do so? What was happening, who were you talking to, what was the outcome?

_____

_____

_____

_____

List the value or values you cared about in each of those instances.

_____

_____

_____

How can being healthy support those values?

_____

_____

_____

_____

How will being wealthy support those values?

_____

_____

_____

_____

Assess Your Joy

Looking to make money for money's sake will provide an empty experience. Many rich people are miserable because the houses, toys, trips around the world, and everything else they've bought didn't bring happiness as they expected. Happiness does not come from the things we own or even the experiences we have. Happiness comes from valuing yourself and contributing to your life in the way you can. I find helping others improve their lives makes me happy, hence writing this book to help anyone who wants to improve their health and wealth fitness. I have had some great experiences in my life, but those are only good for stories at cocktail parties. They don't make me happy. *You do*. Someone actually told me life is boring after you've checked off all your bucket list items (I know, right… champagne problems). Although I still have a ton of bucket list items to work on in my own life, I can imagine having those experiences will not bring internal happiness, at least not forever.

The key to personal happiness is being grateful for where you are, no matter what you have. Having more money or things won't make you happy or fulfilled. You are enough as you are. If you need help finding your gratitude, start a gratitude practice. An easy technique to begin immediately is the gratitude rock. Keep a rock on your desk, and when you notice that rock, briefly think of three to five things you're grateful for currently and three to five things you're thankful for where you'll be in the future.

What are you grateful for where you are? Where you're going?

_____

_____

_____

_____

_____

_____

Of course, money will be a stressor until you reach a minimum level and are no longer worried about the next emergency because you are financially prepared for it. Once you have a minimum financial security level, determine what you want your life to be about to continue working hard. If you're at a financial lifestyle you are happy with and enjoy, there is little reason to continue growing and improving unless your reason for working on yourself is more than money. What makes you happy? If you know the answer to that question, you will keep going because your progress brings you joy, not because you want more money.

> Common Misconception: You've lost money when the market goes down.

Unless you're going to pass away in the next 5-10 years, you'll need to have some money in the market to beat inflation. That means there will be times when you might "lose money." Losing money in the market is like the average American losing weight on a fad diet; it will eventually come back. If you are investing for the long-term, don't sell in a market downturn, and you haven't actually lost anything. Keep adding funds to your investments at regular intervals as usual (see: dollar-cost averaging), and leave your portfolios at the appropriate risk levels. If you're investing for a short period, meaning anything less than two years, your short-term money should be entirely out of the market. Use cash vehicles like money markets, CDs, direct savings, or bank savings accounts until you need the funds.

Consciously Decide to Change

Creating a fit life in both wealth and health requires change for most people. Are you ready for a change? It's easy to start, not so easy to maintain if you're not ready. Andy Andrews says in his book *The Traveler's Gift* that change is easy; it is deciding to change that's hard. He's absolutely right. Once you've determined that something you want to do is worth the work to achieve it, you will do the work. Until you have decided your goal is worth it, you won't want the outcome badly enough. And, that's okay if you don't want the change right now. Maybe you'll have a change of heart, or an external event will send you down a path to make the change later. Maybe you'll realize you don't really want the goal after all.

The point of most importance is you make the decision to change, or not change, consciously. Don't harbor guilt because you aren't doing something you think you should be doing. Either decide you're going to do it or decide you're not and get moving one way or the other. Once you're on board and in the right mindset, you will push through barriers that seemed to exist between where you are now and where you want to be. It's amazing how the shift in mindset and commitment works in both health and wealth when you decide to change.

*Are you authentically ready to make a change in your **health**?*

YES NO

*Are you authentically ready to make a change in your **wealth**?*

YES NO

If you are ready to make the necessary change, sign a conscious statement below to solidify your commitment to yourself.

I, _____, consciously decide to make meaningful change in the following areas: HEALTH WEALTH OTHER

If you are not quite ready to make a change, no problem. Go ahead and sign the conscious statement to continue your inquiry and revisit your commitments later.

I, _____, consciously decide to wait in making meaningful change, but am open to future possibilities and will continue learning so I know what to expect when I am ready to move forward.

If you have others in your life who need to participate in reaching your goals like a roommate, partner, or spouse, make sure they buy-in from the start. Those who have an influence in your life must be aligned. The goals should be mutually agreed upon, and the communication consistent. Short term goals might even take children into account. Remember, those close to you can either support your journey or completely derail it. If the closest people in your life disagree with your priorities, they likely will obstruct your progress consciously or unconsciously. Such frustrations must be avoided from the start.

Is your support network aligned and supportive of your change?

YES NO

Utilize Your Strengths and Avoid Your Weaknesses

Knowing your strengths and weaknesses can help you make decisions in line with your goals before you're in a situation that requires extraordinary self-control. You might not buy small unnecessary goods here and there but splurge on high priced items every so often. Maybe you aren't tempted by chocolate, but you love gummy candies. You know you're able to avoid desserts, but you will gorge yourself mindlessly if near the appetizer tray at a dinner party.

If you have the weaknesses above, what can you do? One, don't go through the gummy candy aisle in the store. Avoiding the aisle altogether removes the temptation. Two, if you do buy yourself a treat for the movies or something, don't buy the bucket of candy. Pay slightly more per piece and buy a small bag. It will keep you from having a stomachache later, I promise. If you're at a party, set up shop away from the food, so you don't eat like a mindless zombie at the appetizer tray. If you have to walk over to the appetizers to get something to eat, you will be less likely to eat without thinking about it.

If you splurge periodically on the finance side, set a dollar amount that any purchase above that amount, you will wait 48 hours before making a purchase. No matter if the salesman says, "you have to buy this right now," wait 48 hours. Most likely, the deal will still be there, or it's coming back around. One-day sales typically last a week or so, and

Black Friday starts on Tuesday these days. You won't miss the deal, and it will keep you from being sold something with urgency when it's not necessary. In the past, I have had clients who literally froze their credit card in a block of ice, so they'd have to wait for the ice to thaw to use their card. I'm not sure how necessary or effective the ice was, but it sure was symbolic of that client's weakness. Clearly, that client knew how to combat their weak points.

Maybe your superpower is you genuinely enjoy eating vegetables. (Who are you, anyway?) What a powerful strength. Veggies are high in fiber and excellent for your health. We'll get to some of that later, but harness your superpower and use it all the time. If you're packing a lunch, throw in some carrots. If you need a snack, grab a pre-filled baggie of cut peppers instead of chips and dip. Thankfully you already like vegetables, so why fight it? Maybe you have always avoided credit cards, even if it was something you did because someone said so, and you listened. What a great habit to start with. Let's capitalize on that and keep you away from the high-interest debts out there

When you can set up an environment that does not fully require your sheer will power or capitalizes on already great habits, you will avoid many of the pitfalls on the road to reaching your goals.

Take a moment now to write down your weak points when it comes to spending and saving:

_____

_____

_____

_____

And your weak points when it comes to food and exercise?

_____

_____

_____

_____

Looking at those above, what are a few avoidances you can use to support your self-control?

_____

_____

_____

_____

What are your strengths and superpowers?

_____

_____

_____

_____

In what ways can you use your strengths to support your money and health habits?

_____

_____

_____

_____

Believe, Act, Repeat

The best way to reach your goals is to start by believing you can. Know you can hit and smash your goals through and through. Believe me. You can. If you set a realistic goal you believe in, have the ability to reach that goal, and believe you can bridge the gap to crush it (in a good way), you will eventually. Then you'll set higher goals and start the process over again.

When you know in your heart of hearts that you can get to where you want to be in finance and health, you will take the first step. Then you'll take a few more, and you'll start seeing results in the direction of your goal. Once you see results, you'll keep taking steps. Then once you hit one of your daily or mid-term goals, set a new one. Once your daily goals become too easy and often hit, increase them. Once you've increased those daily goals, you have to *believe* you can attain the new goals to start making more progress. Belief-action-results-repeat is a wonderful cycle that leads to the life you want in health and wealth.

Gut check: Do you believe what you want is possible?

YES NO

If yes, then what is the first step you could take toward your goal?

_____

_____

If no, then what is something achievable you could strive for? Maybe your other goal will become more believable after you reach a few benchmark goals beforehand.

_____

_____

The method for creating these goals and increasing your motivation toward achieving your dreams is covered in the next chapter on planning.

Embrace Calculated Risk

Risk and reward go hand in hand, and not just in finance. If you want a reward, you almost always have to take some kind of risk. Let's go through a few examples.

Most teenage boys are unsure of themselves and have little confidence. While they work hard to look like they're both sure and confident in themselves. When asking someone out on a date, a boy knows he has to take the first step if he wants the reward of the date. Does he believe the possible humiliation is worth it? If he's too scared to ask, he won't date much. My advice to that shy teen would be to take the risk. Put yourself out there. It is a low-risk action. So, they say no? So what? He's already not going on a date, so he has nothing to lose. Also, there could be any number of reasons they would say no, and many of which don't include him.

For many, the relationship to risk in their portfolio is kind of like that teenage boy looking for dates. Those investors are so afraid of the risk the portfolio might go down in value that they would rather just stay on the sidelines. Sure, you don't have to worry about being rejected, but you'll also never get a date. The problem is you will have a hard time getting to the reward of financial freedom if you're not taking any risk.

Mathematically speaking, you're actually losing money every day you leave your investments on the sidelines in cash. As the cost of your lifestyle goes up with inflation, your bank accounts are not keeping up. The dollar amount may stay the same or even increase slightly, but the amount those dollars buy will go down every time your rent is raised, the cost to fill your gas tank goes up, or the price of milk rises. You have to take reasonable, calculated risks to achieve acceptable returns and get ahead of where you started.

It's more evident with wealth, but in health, you have to take risks as well. To gain muscle, you have to wear out the muscle by pushing it outside your comfort zone, and that takes risk. It is risky to grab a weight and throw it (not literally) above your head; to your body, lifting the weight will feel like a risk. To lose weight, you have to challenge your metabolism with fewer calories. It is risky to go without some of the foods you want because you may make all the healthy choices and forego the delicious, unhealthy food to die anyway from some other cause. To train your heart and increase endurance, you need to push your heart by moving. It is risky to go for a hike, ride your bike to work, even do yoga. You take all kinds of risks, depending on the movements you make. You could get hurt doing almost anything for your health, but you won't get ahead without taking some calculated risk.

Should you jump out of an airplane or sell call options without owning the stock? (If you don't know what I mean by that, you don't need to. Just know it's extremely risky) No. Of course not. I'm saying you must take a calculated risk to have the opportunity for return. The risk level must be appropriate for you and your situation. Please, don't go out of your way to take a risk just to take one. First, determine if the possible reward is worth the downside possibilities for you and your specific situation.

The best part about your mindset is you get to choose what it is. A mindset isn't something that happens to you based on external factors. The power of a positive mindset is the self-talk it creates. Most people know how hard it is to get up at 5 am and drive down the road to the gym to work out before breakfast because most people don't do it. Here's how your mindset will affect your self-talk at 5 am:

- ❏ Negative mindset – I have to get out of my warm bed, drive to the gym, and work hard before I even eat breakfast… I'm going back to bed.

- ❏ Positive mindset – I get to drive to the gym before breakfast to get my workout in and start my day off with productive energy. I can't wait to get my sweat on.

The difference between those two mindsets is a choice to think positively about the benefits of working out early. You can choose your mindset around food, spending, saving, and just about everything else in your life, and your mindset is the first pillar in achieving the outcome you desire.

Planning

Planning is an essential part of the Fit Financial formula. Once you have the right mindset in place, you can start creating the vision and setting your goals. Building out a plan to reach goals is not a natural process for many people. If you don't easily plan, don't let this step scare you. Take the time to walk through the steps laid out in front of you, and before you know it, you'll be on your way.

With any journey, you start by determining where you are now and where you're headed. You may not have a full destination in mind, but you need to know which way to start. Knowing the direction you're heading allows you to know what to pack and what to leave behind. There are checkpoints along the way where you can adjust course before moving on, so don't let being unclear about your future stop you from taking the first step. And, it's okay if you change your destination to a different place while on the way. That's allowed and, it's almost guaranteed as your life changes. Give yourself permission to change while on your journey. Many people choose not to start their first step unless they know exactly where they're headed. In order to start your journey as soon as possible, we need to plan the route for your health and wealth, so you know you're heading in the right direction.

The following steps will guide you through the process of planning. You can use these steps to plan your future in almost any area of your life, but of course, we will be focused on fitness and finances for this book's purposes.

Step #1: <u>Assess the Current Reality</u>, so you know where you are starting.
Step #2: <u>Set Targets</u> to help set the course of your journey.
Step #3: <u>Appoint an AccountabiliBuddy</u> for support, backup, and celebration.
Step #4: <u>Prioritize</u> to align your energy and resources with your goals.
Step #5: <u>Start Taking Steps</u> so you can progress toward your goals.
Step #6: <u>Track Your Progress</u> to course-correct through life's many twists and turns.
Step #7: <u>Adjust as needed</u> when life takes a turn.

None of your desires are going to come quickly and without effort. They will take work and time, focusing in one direction while making more decisions in line with your goals than against them for an extended period. Take the time to plan your path to your goals. It is easier to put a goal out into the universe by simply saying, "I want to retire at age 50" than it is to plan out the steps it will take to get there. It's always amazing to me when someone says, "I had a goal, but the holidays came up, and I ate/spent more than I should have." If I'm not mistaken, the holidays are around the *same time every year*. Thankfully, that makes them easy to plan for. Are you going to eat chicken breast and broccoli for Thanksgiving dinner? Probably not, but you can plan for a cheat day. Work out a bit harder or eat far more consciously than usual the rest of the week when you know you'll be eating a lot one day later in the week. The same goes for the budget. Birthdays and holidays are mostly scheduled at similar times throughout the year. You have a good idea right now where your tough times in the year ahead will be. Plan for them now. If you have a plan only to have one slice of pumpkin pie or talk to your family about a one-on-one gift exchange rather than each family member buying each other family member presents, you may be able to curtail the known hazards.

Planning Step #1 - Assess the Current Reality

To improve your current state of fitness in your wealth, we first determine what that current state is. Be honest, but don't judge yourself. This is about gathering data to inform the start of your journey. You're looking for reality here. It's not about how thrifty or extravagant you've been with spending thus far in life. Where are you right now? Do you spend more than you make? Are you inundated with a large amount of high-interest debt? Whatever the answer is to these questions, it's okay because now we know where we need to do the initial work. You can begin to assess your current reality in several ways:

For your wealth, tap into resources online to **track your expenses**. For a list of resources, you can go to www.fitfinanicalapproach.com. Try not to change the way you spend money while assessing your current lifestyle. We want to get a realistic picture of where your money goes before making changes.

You can also go to www.fitfnancialapproach.com and take the **Fit-Financial Test™** to see your base financial ratios. The ratios evaluated are parameters set by the Certified Financial Planner Board and are generally accepted benchmarks for success. The test will help you determine if you're on track for a financially fit life with where you are currently.

Create your **balance sheet** by capturing everything you have by way of assets and liabilities on one page. Once you have the high-altitude perspective, you'll be able to see your overall net worth as positive or negative. If it's negative, that's okay. This is only a starting place to evaluate where you are and the appropriate path to move forward financially.

We need to do the same thing for your health. What are your assets in fitness? Are you able to run a mile? Are you able to do 20 push-ups? Can you touch your toes? Now, think through your fitness liabilities? Are your hips tight? Are you unable to walk due to injury or other issues? Are you perpetually dehydrated? You may want to use a calorie counter resource to see how many calories you're consuming throughout the day, but you'll need to measure your food for at least three weeks to get the hang of it. You'll learn the approximate size of a 4oz piece of meat or a half cup of vegetables pretty quickly. You'll want to be sure you're getting the quantities of food, and therefore the number of calories, measured accurately at first.

Another tool to use is a body analysis website to input your height, weight, body fat%, and measurements to determine your starting place. See the Fit Financials website resources section for tools you can use to help get started.

Reflect on your current state of fitness in health and wealth. Does anything stand out to you?

_____

_____

_____

_____

_____

_____

_____

_____

_____

Planning Step #2 – Set Your Targets

There are a ton of books on the subject of setting goals. My best advice is to use the method that works for you. For some people, the BHAG's (big hairy audacious goals) from Jim Collins' book *Built to Last* works well. To set a good BHAG, Collins says the goal has to be aligned with your "why," clear and straightforward, and daunting enough to facilitate innovation. For some, if they are a quarter of the way into a goal period and already so far off target there's no possibility of reaching that goal, they will ignore the goal altogether. If that sentiment resonates with you, set some realistic stretch goals you can still attain with some extra work. For instance, if you're starting from scratch and not working out at all right now, maybe your stretch goal is to jog a mile by the end of the month. This will be a target that's not easy when you're not used to setting aside training time, but if it's meaningful, it will get you started. If you're already in decent shape, maybe your goal is to run a half marathon by the end of the summer. This short-term goal is a stretch but realistic and can keep you motivated over the whole goal period. Shorter-term goals in finance are typically at least a quarter or a year down the road. It may be to pay off $5,000 of credit card debt by the end of the year or have $10,000 saved by the end of the quarter. It could be that you want to buy your next car with cash rather than financing it. Whatever your shorter-term goal is, you'll want to make it a stretch but not impossible. A good target is to have a 75% chance of hitting the goals you set in the shorter term.

You must consistently have three different levels of goals:
1. Short-Term Goals: Daily or weekly activity targets to reach a one to six-month ultimate goal.
2. Medium-Term Goals:
   ❏ Health – One to three years in time.
   ❏ Wealth – Three to five years out.
3. Lifelong Goal List: These goals are not necessarily tied to a timeline, but you want to accomplish them at some point in your life. They may move to your short- or medium-term list when you're ready.

Lifelong Goals

Start by defining your **lifelong goals.** These goals aren't necessarily what you want to be when you grow up, and they will never be set in stone. These lifelong goals are something you want to achieve at some point in your lifetime. Some say they want to complete an Iron Man triathlon one day, and many want to donate large sums of money to their schools or a non-profit. Even though these goals aren't tied to a specific timeline, they are still priorities to plan for. Don't worry. You can always change them if you want. Many young people are paralyzed by the idea they have to pick something and be that something forever and ever and EVER. You don't. You can always change who you are and who you want to be in life. The idea old dogs cannot learn new tricks is unsubstantiated. Old dogs may not want to learn new tricks, but they sure can. They just have to be properly motivated by a goal that matters. If you define a goal that aligns with your "why," even if it takes some work to hit it, you will take steps toward that goal regardless of age. That means you can choose what you want to be now with little recourse if you change your idea later.

These lifelong goals can be as big as you want. For a while now, mom's everywhere have been saying, "you can be anything." It's probably somewhat true if you're willing to put in the effort and catch the right breaks at the right times. But really. Dream big. There are no wrong answers, and you're not going to be judged for wanting too much or too little from life. It's your life, and you get to choose the adventure that fits you.

Take a minute to focus on the inquiries you started in the earlier chapters. Again, there are no wrong answers.

What do you want most out of life?

_____

_____

_____

_____

_____

_____

_____

Why do you want what you want? Remember - your "Why" will keep you moving when things get tough.

_____
_____
_____
_____
_____

How would you feel if you were able to accomplish it?

_____
_____
_____
_____
_____

With longer-term life goals, it's helpful to keep them in front of you, reminding you to stay on track with your decision making and thinking about your dream often enough to make it a reality. If you think of your goal every day, you will make decisions in line with your goal and have a higher likelihood of actually reaching it one day. For example, when preparing for a trip to Hawaii, you could keep a picture of the beach taped to the pantry door. That picture will remind you to stay on track when looking to snack. You could also create a background on your phone or computer to bring your goal top-of-mind. You can even use countdown apps for goals with a date of completion. One client keeps a sticky note on her dashboard; she looks at it every day to remind her not to impulse buy. She tells me it helps her refrain from going through drive-throughs, helping both her health and wealth stay on track. Bonus.

Once you've made up your mind about your future, don't second-guess yourself. Work toward becoming the person you would need to be in order to reach that goal. On the path to becoming that person, you'll learn more about yourself. You'll learn what you like and don't like about being more fit in finance and health. Maybe, while training for a marathon, you determine you don't really like running much. In the meantime, you find you enjoy biking, so you may want to change your goal to complete the Triple Bypass bike race in Colorado. When you change your goals after learning more about yourself on your path to success, those changes aren't second-guessing your future. They will be clarifying. Your new future goal is an adjustment, of course, and the progress you have made so far will continue to be beneficial while on your new path.

Medium-Term Goals

Once your lifelong goal is set, you can take a step back. Look at your current situation and evaluate what significant next steps to take toward your lifelong goal. The big steps needed will instruct your **medium-term goals**. For example, if you need to learn a new skill or gain a new perspective, would school help? If a degree or certification won't get you closer, where could you learn what you need to approach the lifelong goal? In my case, I have a degree in finance, but I did not have any experience helping people enact change in their lives. Although I always knew I wanted to be a financial planner, I was looking for the right firm to work for. The search proved harder than expected, so while looking for the right firm, I applied for a job as a trainer as I knew a trainer helped people change their lives for the better. I learned and honed the skills of helping people better themselves and their lives as a trainer.

Be strategic...plan ahead. Think of how you could get one step closer to your lifelong goal. This medium-term goal could be something you're not able to work on right away. There may be a few interim steps to get there. That's okay. Write those steps down, too. That's the idea of a good plan: One goal leads to the next one until we get where we ultimately want to be. If you're having trouble coming up with the interim goals to reach your lifelong objectives, ask yourself why you can't complete your lifelong goals right now? Typically, whatever you say when answering that question will instruct the medium-term goals to work toward to get one step closer to achieving your life goals. With your interim goals in place, you can then define the short-term goals.

Make a quick list of potential medium-term goals that come to mind. Given the current realities of your life, what medium-term actions will get you one step closer to your lifelong goals?

_____

_____

_____

_____

_____

_____

_____

_____

Short-Term Goals

The **short-term goal setting** is focused on activity. The question to continually ask yourself is: What daily activity will get me closer to my mid and long-term goals? The action could be something as simple as reading leadership books for fifteen minutes every morning. This has been a short-term goal of mine off and on for years. I know I need to be a better leader to achieve my long-term goals, so I will probably continue working on that goal for an entire lifetime. If you're writing a book, your short-term goal could be to write for three hours a week. Your goal could be to go for a walk during lunch three days a week.

When you do the work of self-discovery through answering the questions in this book and knowing what you want to accomplish in life, you can then set meaningful goals. The idea of setting a goal is to give you a target to aim for. If you don't hit it, aim again. Don't feel disappointed in yourself for not hitting your daily goal *every* day. I've found it motivating to set goals I can hit 70-80% of the time. These goals stretch me, but they aren't too much of a stretch that I give up on tracking after missing one week. If a goal doesn't stretch or challenge you at all, it's also not motivating. Setting a step goal you can hit before leaving your home in the morning for work will not motivate you to track your steps every day. Challenging but not impossible is the key to daily motivational goals.

With your daily goals helping you reach the next step toward mid-term goals, which is the next step toward your lifetime goal, all your motivation will be building in the same direction. Keeping that long-term goal in front of you will keep you motivated to reach the daily goals and, eventually, each step along the way. As we reach more steps, we are motivated to go for another step, then another, and so on. Progress leads to results, which leads to motivation, which leads to more progress. This is the upward spiral we can all take advantage of to improve our life in fitness and finances.

One step at a time is the way you'll make any journey in your life. Make your list of short-term goals. Given the current realities of your life, what daily actions will get you one step closer to your medium-term and lifelong goals?

_____

_____

_____

_____

_____

_____

_____

_____

_____

_____

Planning Step #3 – Appoint an AccountabiliBuddy

It helps me to talk through the next few weeks, months, and years of my plan with someone who cares. For years, my wife and I have gone on walks together to discuss long-term life and financial goals. Our walking partners have changed through the years from a dog on a leash to one kid in a stroller, two kids in a stroller…now three on bikes. These days, we usually talk about our goals between yelling at children to "Watch out for that car." Our future has changed as our life has changed, but we still discuss our plans while on walks.

You'll also want to have an accountability partner or financial planner to support you in fulfilling your plan and discuss steps along the way. Your choice of a buddy could be the difference between making progress on your goals and giving up in three months. There are a few things to consider when looking for a buddy for your financial and fitness goals.

- ❏ <u>Choose a buddy who will tell you the truth.</u> This is not taking a friend to coffee to vent about your life. This is an "AccountabiliBuddy" who feels responsible for helping you achieve your desired future. If they show up to your financial check-up, notice your new car in the parking lot (the one you didn't need), and say nothing, find someone else immediately.
- ❏ <u>Work with a buddy who has similar long-term goals</u>. When you're working out to gain muscle, you're not going to hit the gym with a marathon runner trying to decrease their split times. If you want to pay off your house, but they want to buy a vacation home, you could get bad advice and support on your journey just because of a differing worldview and life priorities. That doesn't make their view or yours wrong. They are just incompatible as your AccountabiliBuddy.
- ❏ <u>Find someone who is further along than you are or at least in the same place in their life</u>. You don't want to find a gym buddy who is sitting on the couch every day. You need someone to motivate you to keep going even when it gets tough. When you're whining about wanting to go out to dinner or on a spending spree, you want someone ahead of you saying, "stay the course, you can do it, and you'll be happy you did." You won't listen to their advice if your buddy is lazy behind you because you know they haven't done the work themselves.

While working with a buddy to reach your financial goals, the logistics are similar in the health world. Meet more often at first to get on the right track. Set up your cash flow and how you will monitor your progress. Share your short-term goals and come up with a plan to start holding each other accountable. Then meet as often as you need to get going in the right direction. As your new lifestyle becomes less of a challenge and more of a habit, you two can meet less often to course-correct. It is far easier to keep momentum than it is to gain momentum in the first place. That's science. Newton's law of inertia states that an object in motion tends to stay in motion and an object at rest tends to stay at rest. The law applies to your health and wealth just as much as it does to a ball rolling downhill.

When you're a bit further downfield and start hitting some of your goals, celebrate with your buddy. They are an integral part of your success, and they deserve the reward just as much as you do. They'll also be committed to celebrating in a way that keeps you on track. Although one day won't kill your goals, you don't want to go on an all-out ice cream binge for a week every time you hit a medium- or long-term goal.

List 3-5 people you know who could make for a good Accountabili-Buddy:

1. _____

2. _____

3. _____

4. _____

5. _____

If you feel inspired, go ahead and call your top pick and pop the "will you be my AccountabiliBuddy" question. If you need to sit with this decision for a few days, by all means, do so. Call them up when you are clear and ready to go.

Planning Step #4 - Prioritize What You Want

The reason clients most often say they don't like to use a budget for cash flow or a caloric intake plan is because the clients believe the budgets are restrictive. Yes, they can *feel* that way when you restrict your cash flow or make different food choices, but the restriction doesn't have to be a bad thing. It can also feel empowering. Cash flow management is not just a blanket recommendation to spend less money and cut out what you love. You can still eat what you enjoy as well. The true goal of fitness change for health and wealth is **aligning your choices with your priorities**.

Let's say you love to lift heavy weights and need extra protein plus other supplements to reach your fitness goals. Great, but the workout supplement industry is not a multi-billion-dollar industry because they're cheap. Understand what you are giving up to afford to buy expensive products. Supplementation is covered in detail later, but you should not cut *anything* out of your budget that you love. To reach your financial goals, you will have to give up some things you don't really care about to keep the ones you love.

The best way to rank your priorities is to assess your current budget. When tracking a budget, people tend to spend differently. Remember, to assess your actual reality of spending, don't change your spending habits during the tracking period. Once you've had enough time to evaluate where your money goes, take a few minutes to assess how you feel about those spending choices. If at any time you think to yourself, "I spend how much on that?!?," you know it's not a priority. Some clients will rank their list of expense categories from 1-5. If you find you're spending a larger percentage of your funds on consumption that isn't ranked a three or higher, consider changing your spending habits in that area. Simple, right? If you spend $10 a day on eating out at the cafe next to your office, and you think, "I could make a $1.00 peanut butter and jelly with carrots and be just as happy," then stop eating out. Start packing a lunch.

On the other hand, if you're spending $120 per month on your favorite yoga classes and those classes are essential for maintaining your lifestyle, then, by all means, keep that membership in your budget for now. You could potentially look for a different, cheaper studio. Or evaluate whether you are attending class often enough to get $120 of value from them. Maybe you could switch to a punch card arrangement where you only pay for the classes you attend? But you don't need to get rid of your yoga expense completely.

Here is an example of what a spending tracker could look like for your monthly expenses:

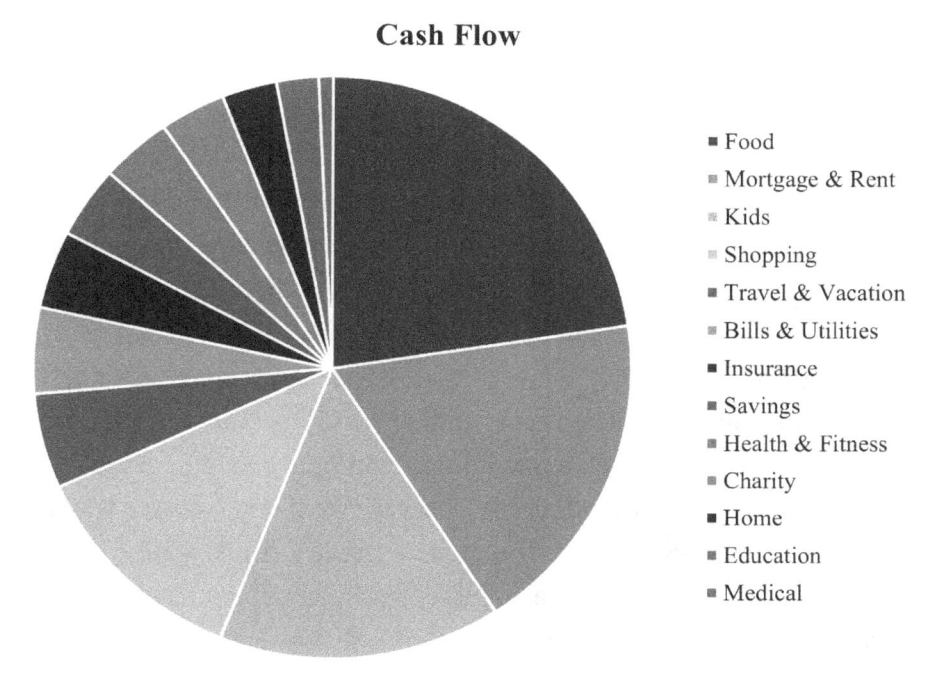

Cash Flow

- Food
- Mortgage & Rent
- Kids
- Shopping
- Travel & Vacation
- Bills & Utilities
- Insurance
- Savings
- Health & Fitness
- Charity
- Home
- Education
- Medical

Take the list of spending categories and line them up next to the list of priorities you created earlier to verify the two lists are in line with each other.

You can also do this exercise with your diet as well. Once you track your food for a little while, you'll notice consumption themes. You can use the same 1-5 priority ranking system to determine how foods rank in your current diet. Please, don't rank your food intake by what you think society would tell you is good and bad. Rank your priorities by the foods you value. When going through this exercise for myself, I realized I love sweet potatoes, and thankfully they are a healthy food. I also determined I don't enjoy chocolate as much as I thought I did. I'm more of a salty snack person. How interesting. Now I know I don't have to waste my calories on chocolate, and I'm more conscious that I don't care if I eat it. However, if there's a bowl of salty tortilla chips with salsa, I'm probably going to partake. Typically, people don't realize how they feel about their foods; they mindlessly eat just because the food is there.

Once you've completed the assessment exercise, you will feel a bit better about all this. You've taken an essential step in understanding yourself and applying that information to your cash flow and calorie intake. The best way to determine what people prioritize is to look at where they spend their time and money. People who don't pay attention to their expenses and food will spend excessive amounts and eat many things they could care less about.

When I went through this exercise years ago for my finances, I gained enormous insight. I was spending WAY too much on workout supplements (hence the example above) and hair care (for a guy who has a pretty straightforward hairdo). Also, we went out to coffee way too often to pay over $5 per trip. To course-correct, I found a new barbershop right away, and I bought a single-cup coffee maker. Instead of five-dollar-cups of coffee, we drink thirty-five-cent cups and bring them with us. We still go out to coffee from time to time to treat ourselves, but not nearly as often as before. I then researched the supplements I had sold to clients as a personal trainer. There are some great resources out there. Use third-party, non-affiliated research to find unfiltered information on the available supplements in the marketplace. Please do your research for yourself, but I found my supplements were not tested and had no proof they do what they said they would do. After testing on myself by continuing my workouts and cutting out the extra powders, I realized I saw little to no effect from all the extra expense, so I cut out everything except a few highly researched and verified supplements that actually worked. I took my workout supplement budget from $250-300 per one month to $30 per three months, freeing up more than $2,880 a year. I still prioritize my health and fitness, of course, but I don't need to pay for anything that's not adding value to my style of workouts.

Every dollar counts. If $200+ per month doesn't sound like a lot, because you make a ton of money, that's great. But think of what else you could do with those dollars, whether for yourself or someone else. After you've gone through these exercises and aligned your spending with your priorities, you won't feel restricted; you'll feel liberated. Now you're making decisions based on what matters to you and what doesn't, rather than blindly spending money. That's a powerful position to be in and a great place to start your journey.

The Priority Checklist
- ❏ Make a list of all expenses.
- ❏ Rank them 1-5 in order of importance to you.
- ❏ Cut expenses that are of no importance.
- ❏ Look for any cost-effective alternatives for your critical expenditures.

Planning Step #5 – Start Taking Steps

Now you know where you want to go with your health and wealth fitness. You know your current situation, and you know what you care most about. Now all you have left to do is work the plan. Take the first steps and push forward. It's okay to change your direction while on this path. It's not okay to stop. Think through the mid-term goals your path to the big, lifetime goal. Also, think through what you're going to do when you have an unexpected health issue or expense that sets you back on your progress. Speed bumps like these are inevitable, so think through them ahead of time. They are less likely to slow you down long term if you know how you'll react. What are you going to do when you don't feel motivated to work out today? What will you do when you forget your lunch on the kitchen counter? Do you need to have a backup plan like a second alarm clock or canned chili at your desk? (Yes, canned chili has a ton of salt, but it's cheaper and better for you than a burger across the street from the office.)

What speedbumps could derail your progress? How could you prepare for them?

_____

_____

_____

_____

_____

_____

_____

Remember, a goal is meant to send you in a direction. Let's say you planned to pay off your house over the next ten years. You get to year eight, and your spouse says something along the lines of "I have the offer of a lifetime to work for XYZ Company in ABC city. We can't pass this up." Don't come back to them with, "well, we really need to stay on course here until we pay off our house." Your partner wouldn't feel very supported. Although you may ultimately decide to stay put and keep working on the plan, have a conversation about the opportunity and evaluate where you are and whether this is a good enough reason to detour for a bit. Perhaps, the opportunity will move your plan forward exponentially. It may be a good time for you to take a walk.

What first step are you going to take today? This week? What's your second step? When?

_____

_____

_____

_____

_____

_____

_____

Planning Step #6 - Track your progress

While on your personal journey to a healthy, wealthy life, you will have times when you feel like you're crushing it. You're saving a ton of money every month; you're working out every day. Life is good. You'll also have those times when you feel as though you're in a rut and nothing is going your way. I hate to tell you this, but either way, you're wrong. Regardless of where you are on your path, your feelings have little to do with your progress.

Every so often, you must step out of the day-to-day to evaluate your plan. Is it no longer serving you? Is it working against the goals of those closest to you? Does it need to change? If so, change it; you don't have to adhere to your plan or even your goals permanently. Your relationships are not served by forcing your plan on those you love. Make sure that your plan continues to fit into your priorities and the priorities of your support network.

Only when you track your progress will you verify where you are and how you're progressing through your financial or physical journey. Keep a log of your workouts. Periodically take measurements of your waist, legs, arms, chest, body fat, etc. Every once in a while, take a step back and review the results compared to the past. Record the number of push-ups, pull-ups, squats, and crunches you can do in one minute without rest. Track what makes sense for you. If you're trying to gain muscle, you will measure different areas than someone trying to run their first marathon. You need to track your progress, so you can look back when you don't feel motivated to see how far you've actually come. Seeing where you've been helps focus on where you're going. When you are not feeling great about where you are in health or fitness, pull out your log and see the progress you have made. You'll feel re-energized to keep going.

Common Misconception: My home always goes up in value

No, it doesn't. You just don't notice the price fluctuations because there isn't a quarterly statement showing you exactly what someone would pay you for your house each quarter. Companies like Zillow help us estimate the value of our home at any given time, as they estimate the values of homes based on comparable home sales in the same neighborhood. The problem is these services can only provide ballpark figures. Their numbers are off-base because their algorithms don't consider unique selling features, conditions of the homes, or other localized factors. Because there are thousands of buyers and sellers of the same security, or stock, on a major exchange, we know exactly what people are willing to pay for that stock on any given day. Your home gets sold once every few years, with only one buyer and one seller at any given time, each with their own personal life circumstances at play; therefore, it's hard to quantify what the real estate is worth.

Yes, the peaks and valleys in real estate are not as severe as they can be in the stock market, but that doesn't mean they don't exist. We forget so quickly, sometimes. Remember the 2006 housing bubble that burst in 2007, causing an economic recession for years to come? Many families across America who were foreclosed on their homes had to short sell (the name for selling a home worth less than the outstanding loan) to get out of a bad loan they could not afford. Many declared bankruptcy. Real estate can lose value. Treat it accordingly.

On the financial side, measure and keep a running tab of your net worth and other metrics. Measure what you have in emergency funds, debt, retirement accounts, family vacation funds, etc. Are you trying to pay down debt? Then keep track of your total debt. Are you saving for a specific retirement number? Track your retirement account totals over time, so you can reflect on your investment totals and the money you've saved one step at a time. Review your progress quarterly and reconsider priorities annually.

Make it easier to track. If you don't want to gather numbers manually, there are apps for every possible measurement you could want to track in health and wealth. A website like Mint.com tracks all of your bills, budgeting, loans, investments, and more all in one place. Apps like MyFitnessPal keep a running tab of your caloric intake and calories burned. You could also create spreadsheets to customize what you track and not deal with the ads. Whatever you choose to do, keep a record of where you've been, so you know how far you are along the journey. When you feel like you're in a rut and not making progress, look back at how far your small steps have taken you to this point. When you are on fire and feel like you're crushing your goals, check your measurements to verify you are indeed chugging along. Don't think of this as a sprint or even a marathon. Picture a lifestyle you can continue to put one foot in front of the other as you enjoy the scenery. Then take healthy, consistent steps to live into that lifestyle. Track your progress with verifiable data, and you will be focused and stepping in the right direction.

Great work. At this point, your mindset is positive about your future. You've taken the time to plan your initial direction with checkpoints along the way. You have measured yourself, determined your net worth, and set your priorities as a baseline for your progress. You have already done so much work for your fitness and financial future; just going through these mindset and planning steps places you in a position to better your life. Now, it's time to walk your path to health and wealth through habit creation and modification.

Habits

The habits needed to create a healthy and wealthy future are built on the same foundations, and if used correctly, they can significantly improve your life. Charles Duhigg states in his book *The Power of Habit: Why We Do What We Do in Life and Business,* "typically, people who exercise, start eating better and becoming more productive at work... They use their credit cards less frequently and say they feel less stressed." If you're going to improve one of these aspects of your life, you may as well use the combined benefit shown in the research and enhance both.

Habits are the name of the game. The method of creating positive habits won't help you get rich quickly or immediately drop weight; you will learn easy-to-sustain ways to improve your life over time. This book is your guide to show you the path to building these sustainable habits, but you still have to walk the path and follow them. The only way to reach the other end of the path where your health and wealth goals lie is to keep walking. If you successfully develop the habits, the positive actions will become part of your lifestyle, and as you continue the practices over time, you will see a complete life transformation. The change won't happen all at once, and it won't necessarily be comfortable all the time, but living into the lifestyle you build will create the life you've always wanted. You will feel like you earned it, like you did it yourself… because you did.

While the Fit Financial formula is a guide for implementing change, there is no magic formula to success. No one piece of information will give you everything you want in health and wealth. If someone promised you if you do "just this one thing," you'll have a six-pack, a tight butt, or you'll levitate, they are selling you a load of something. Don't buy it. There is no magic bean to eat. No micronutrient will make you shed weight immediately. There are no get-rich-quick schemes. Any investment that has the opportunity for great gain is packaged with a significant risk of loss. If it were easy, everyone would do it. It's not, and they don't. There are no short cuts. You can't take a shuttle or skip to the end.

There are a few rules you can use to make this journey a bit easier, however. If you can follow these rules, you can make your short-term change into a habit, and if you can sustain the habit long enough, you'll make it a lifestyle. Once you've made your short-term change into a lifestyle, you won't be able to do anything but aggressively strive for your goals. This is the key. Don't try to take the easy way out. Don't try to get out at all. Just habitually assemble a financially and physically fit lifestyle you can embrace and enjoy for the rest of your life. Although you can visualize your objective, you'll realize it isn't entirely about the destination. If you hike to the top of a mountain, but you fail to take a look around on your way up, you will miss the best part of the day. Sure, the mountain views are gorgeous at the top, but the life, views, people, and experiences along the way are even better. The best part of this whole journey is experienced when you realize you're having fun living a healthy and wealthy lifestyle. Once walking the path has become fun, you've already succeeded, even if you have a distance to cover remaining.

So… keep walking.

Reward - Cue - Ritual

Use this three-step approach to building and maintaining a healthy habit. In Duhigg's book on habits, he references the science behind a habit in your life. Whether it's a healthy or unhealthy habit, it consists of three parts: the cue, the ritual, and the reward. The cue is the action or situation that tells your brain to act. For example, getting out of the shower is the cue to start getting ready for your day. The routine, or ritual, is the action triggered by the cue. In day to day life, we often engage in unconscious rituals like the steps we go through to get ready in the morning. If I change the order of my routine, often I'll forget one of the steps. Finally, the reward is whatever the brain gets out of the routine. In the case of your morning prep, the reward is not having to consciously think of everything you do to get ready every single day. The habit saves brain space.

Smoking is one of the most challenging habits to break. A smoker with a cue of driving home from work begins a ritual of pulling out a cigarette and lighting it up without even realizing what they're doing, as soon as they pull out of the parking lot. The reward is the quick burst of nicotine their brain craved. This is an excellent example of an unhealthy, unconscious habit. Many former smokers say the mental trigger to reach for a cigarette, not the nicotine addiction, is the most difficult part of quitting smoking. For an awfully long time after stopping smoking, they still reached—without thinking—for a cigarette when their cue was triggered, even though the cigarettes weren't there.

What are some of the habit cues, rituals, and rewards in your life that happen automatically?

_____

_____

_____

_____

_____

_____

_____

Creating New Habits

Building a healthy habit doesn't take as much effort when you make a conscious decision to follow a method that works. It takes consistency. If it feels hard at first, you won't stick with it for the time necessary to see real change. Utilizing the three steps of a habit, we can engineer healthy rituals to create progress toward goals or replace the unhealthy habits holding you back. By following the conscious, healthy habit creation process, you can make it easier to maintain consistency over a longer time. Just as you don't think about your morning routine while you are going through your steps unconsciously, you can create that same level of ease while designing healthy habits around your health and wealth.

The habit engineering process has three-steps and works for both habit creation and modification. By being intentional about the different aspects of a habit, you can construct your routines consciously rather than unconsciously falling into your habits over time. The steps to create healthy habits are design reward, determine cue, and simplify ritual. Let's walk through using the three-step process to form a new, healthy habit.

Step 1: Design Rewards
The whole purpose of a habit is to reward your brain from the action, so the first step is evaluating those mental rewards. You have your goals and your why, so look to creating habitual rewards to work toward these goals. Some of these mental rewards could be the time saved in the morning by setting aside tomorrow's meals and snacks the night before or the pride you feel after paying your credit card off in full every month. At this point, all you need is a list of habit rewards that will help you reach your goals:

What are some of the mental rewards you'd like to add to your routine?

_____

_____

_____

_____

_____

Step 2: Determine Cues
The second step in forming a new habit that will get you to your goal life is to determine your cues to implement. Cues are crucial to our brains. Without them, we would have to think about every decision and action we take in a day. When you get in the shower, you don't have to think about

whether you're going to clean your hair, then your face and body. You just do it, and your brain thanks you as it didn't have to do any heavy lifting. In the second step, the goal is to use the efficiency (or laziness if you want to think of it that way) of our brains to our advantage. If the reward you're adding is drinking more water, all you have to do is link drinking water with something you do several times a day. You could pair it with going to the bathroom at work. Every time you get up to use the restroom, you could stop by the water cooler to fill up your water bottle before you head back to your desk. If the reward you need to add is checking your cash flow every week, you could set a calendar reminder that sends its own unique ring tone. You could also tie checking your cash flow with taking your trash to the curb on trash day, during your weekly goal check-in walk with your spouse, or any other task you have to complete once a week. Evaluate how often you need to receive the mental reward to remain consistent toward your goal. You can find cues in your current routines that match the necessary timing to give you the best opportunity to complete the ritual. Make a conscious effort to complete the habit loop at first. Completing the whole habit loop – cue, routine, reward – for a few weeks will ingrain that cue into your mind's subconscious. You won't even have to think about the rest of the steps anymore.

What cues could you use to initiate rituals that work toward your wanted rewards?

_____

_____

_____

_____

Step 3: Simplify Ritual

The third step is to review the routine and make it as easy as possible to implement. If you're trying to instill a new habit like working out before work, you could set your alarm across the room and set your gym clothes right next to it. You'll have to walk across the room to turn off the alarm, which forces you to wake up, and if your gym clothes are right there, you're more likely to put them on and start exercising. The ritual is something you do without thinking, so make it as easy as possible for your brain to follow the steps. Don't try to do too much at first. Some may try to start their habit ritual by waking up early to write, meditate, exercise, and more on day one. They end up sticking to it for a week, if that, and dropping out soon after. You must ingrain the basic ritual before making it too complicated. Start with the number one goal you'd like to accomplish. Once you get that routine down, you can always add to it, but take it one step at a time for the best results.

How could you make your rituals as easy as possible to implement? If there are multiple rewards you'd like to accomplish simultaneously, which is the most important to implement first?

_____

_____

_____

_____

_____

_____

Modifying an Existing Habit

Now let's look at the reward, cue, and ritual process for modifying an existing habit that takes you away from your goals. For instance, is the nicotine fix from smoking a cigarette something that gets you closer to the healthy, long life you want to live? No, of course not.

Step 1: Change Current Rewards

In the first step, look at the current habits in your life and ask if they are generating rewards that help you reach that life you've envisioned? If the answer is no, then ask if they're worth it? For some of the rewards, the answer will be no, and we can work on getting rid of those. On the other hand, you may have a few you feel are worth it, even though they take you away from your goals. That's okay. Remember: the way to your best life is not to cut out *all* the things you enjoy and sacrifice them for your future. Know that the action will take you away from your goals, and enjoy it in moderation.

Are the current rewards in your habit cycles working toward or against your goals? If against your goals, will you keep them in moderation or eliminate them altogether?

Reward	Toward/Away from goals	Eliminate/Moderate

Step 2: Modify Cues
The second step is modifying the cues that kick off your habit ritual. Just knowing it's unhealthy to snack before bed won't stop you from doing it if you're caught in a habit loop. If your goal is to stop snacking before bed, you can find whatever the cue is that sends you off to the pantry and change it. Suppose you recognize that you're heading to the pantry between episodes while binge-watching your favorite show. In that case, you can either start watching your show in a different part of the house where you can't get to the pantry and back in the few seconds you have between episodes or grab some herbal tea instead of a snack. Maybe you could read a book like this one? Or you could dive into a new series on a streaming service that doesn't have commercials. Once you identify your cue, you will notice when it is affecting your life, and that knowledge gives you the power to change the habit.

In the smoking example, the cue is starting the car and driving away. It leads to unconsciously reaching for a cigarette. To break the habit, the former smoker has to make the routine more of a conscious effort by parking in a different lot or exiting a different way after work. If you know that driving home on your usual route will prompt you to stop for a take-out dinner, consciously choose to go home a different way. You can save yourself the money and the calories. Evaluate your cues and change them as needed to get out of the habit cycle.

What cues set off the rituals that take you away from your goals? How could you modify them or eliminate them from your life?

_____

_____

_____

_____

Step 3: Improve or Remove Ritual

The third step, once again, is to evaluate the rituals and set yourself up for success by removing or improving the ritual. Having willpower when at the gas station may be all a former smoker needs to stop smoking. If they remove the ritual of going inside the station, they won't buy cigarettes and won't have anything to reach for when pulling out of the parking lot. If your habit is one you'd like to change, like snacking too often on Cheez Doodles, you only have to have willpower at the time of purchasing the Doodles to remove the temptation from your life. You could also take the time to set up easy-to-grab, pre-packaged, healthy snacks. This way, if you really can't resist walking to the fridge, at least you've got some veggie snacks instead of something with little to no nutritional value.

How could you modify your life to make it easy to improve or remove your rituals that lead away from your goals?

_____

_____

_____

_____

_____

_____

Make habit-changing easy on yourself by taking advantage of the inherent efficiency of the brain. This three-step process of reward, cue, and ritual can help you change or create just about any habit you need to reach your long-term goals. If you can set aside the brief amount of time it takes to evaluate your current and missing habits, design your life around them, and stick with them long enough to ingrain the new habits, your brain will go into auto-pilot, taking you right to your desired destination.

Make Small, Meaningful Changes Over Time

When making positive changes in your health and wealth, you will likely feel excited. That's great. Just don't bite off more than you can chew. Take easy steps at first with everything in moderation, even good things. You've probably heard these sayings a million times and dismissed them as just another load of crap, but these rote mantras speak to the truth of how our bodies and minds work together to make meaningful change in our lives. Don't cut out an entire macronutrient like carbohydrates or fat to lose weight unless it is for a short period of time. Don't cut your overall calories too much; your body could reject the change and, for survival, slow your metabolism and hold on to your bodyfat more than usual, which completely defeats the purpose of cutting back on your caloric intake. If you do one of the many cleanses that eliminate particular or all foods besides water, you can make the change far too hard and create a physiological situation where your cravings will become hard to resist. Once the cleanse is over—I have seen this time and time again—people go right back to eating and living the way they did beforehand. Or worse, they binge. This is not the way to see results.

Please don't cut your budget so deep you're not having fun; you'll never last on a track like that. Not to mention, you won't enjoy the journey. If you can't stay on track with your cash flow for long periods, you'll never reach your goals. If you can currently save $300 per month after some cash flow prioritization, start there. Don't try to jump right to saving $1,000 a month and eat instant noodles three nights a week; you'll never be able to stick to that program. Likewise, don't lace up your new running shoes and head out the door on a five-mile run the first day; you will hurt yourself and be unable to continue to day two.

As an overly excited person when it comes to change, I've been known to gear up and try to change everything as fast as possible. I like to see significant results. Of course, we all quickly burn-out when confronting too much change at one time—don't burn yourself out. The best course of action is to take one step at a time. Change the thing that will get you the biggest bang for your buck, then move to the next change with the largest impact, then the next.

This should not be a painful exercise. Take your time. Change is uncomfortable, but it should also be manageable. Life is about progress, not perfection. Start with any change by keeping it simple. Begin with a bite-sized decision that will get you started down the path. If you're at square one, evaluate your situation for habits you can change easily without disrupting your life. Maybe start waking up 15 minutes earlier than usual to stretch and drink a glass of water. You could simply cut out a few unnecessary expenses to start reducing your cash outflow; you won't even notice. You can get to pushing yourself little by little after that. Action leads to more action, so you can take a second and third step after you've fully incorporated the first. The goal is to make a change, not to be perfect. The key at this stage is to start; take the first step. The second step will come after the first. The third will come after the second, and so on after that. (Funny how that works.)

Get in the habit of taking simple actions. How do you eat an elephant? One bite at a time. Maybe first you cut out sodas. Then work on cutting back on the fast-food stops. Then add more vegetables into your life. Then work on portion control. Then... You see where this is going.

Finances are the same. Start with something easy. Rearrange your debts to lower your monthly bills. Then take the monthly amount you saved and build up your cash savings. Then pay down more of the debt and add a percentage point to your 401k at work. Then pay off the debt, take the funds you were using for payments, and add it to other investments. Start a vacation fund to save for trips ahead of time instead of putting them on cards. Again, you see where this is headed.

Strategies for health and wealth improvement are covered later, but the point is to have a mindset of change by knowing your "why," deciding to change, and planning your habits for one step in front of the other to see real progress over time. It won't happen all at once, and when it does happen that quickly, it's probably not long-lived. We're cultivating a lifestyle.

Common Misconception: Easy results are not so easy

Some studies have shown that someone who wins the lottery or receives a sum of money that wasn't earned will have purchased a vehicle within 21 days. Within 18 months, the recipients are out of money and in the same or worse position on average than before they had the windfall. *Eighteen months?!? Are you kidding me?* In the same vein, if you cut out carbohydrates while trying to diet, you're going to lose 7-10 lbs. in the first two weeks. You know why? Carbohydrates hold water in your body. Congratulations, you dropped water, not fat. I'm guessing that wasn't your goal. On average, those who drop weight that fast will gain it all back or more within a short period.

Stick with Your Chosen Path

Making decisions quickly and changing your mind slowly is advice from Andy Andrews in his book, *The Traveler's Gift*. This is excellent advice for all aspects of life. We often make a change and stick with it only for a few days, weeks, maybe even a few months. Eventually, many will look at the short-term results and determine that the effort isn't worth the return, and they choose to try something new. In most areas of life, and especially in health and wealth, results take time to start showing. We work so hard with little to show, only to see a landslide of results once we reach the tipping point. Many people change strategies *just before* results start to show.

There's a fable of a man who traveled across the country to find gold in the 1840s. He dug and dug and dug on his land, convinced there was gold down there somewhere. Later, gold diggers discovered that he was less than three feet away from hitting pay dirt when he gave up and traveled back to where he came from. The fable has been recounted many times with different locations and names, it's most likely not a true story, but the principle is appropriate. Don't give up and change course just before your results start showing, and you achieve what you've been working for.

Have you ever tried, say, Tabata style workouts for a week, then tested yoga for a couple of weeks, then moved on to a spin class and decided that's not working, so you started looking for something new? Depending on your goals, any of those workout routines could be the right one for you, but you would have to stick with them for at least a couple of *months* to see any viable data that could inform whether you're on the right path. If you just blindly switch from one program to the next because the workout doesn't "feel" right, you could be missing out on the right style of workout for your body.

The same advice is true for your finances. Pick a strategy that will help you reach your goals and stick with it for a while. Consider that 'a while' in finances is a lot longer than 'a while' in fitness. The person who switches their portfolio to last year's high-performing investments will most likely lag behind someone who sticks to their plan over the long haul. The economy tends to work in cycles. That means certain areas of the economy will grow, then shrink a bit, then grow, and shrink, over and over again. That's why economists call it the economic cycle. There's no real rhyme or reason to the cycles, so no one is actually able to predict the area of the market in which a growth spurt will happen and when. However, picking the sector that just went through a growth cycle is *not* a good strategy to reach your long-term goals. Whether you choose a risk-appropriate, globally diversified portfolio in the style of Modern Portfolio Theory to hold over a long period while rebalancing annually, or you select an active fund manager to try to beat the market over periods of time, give the strategy a chance to work over an entire market cycle. A full cycle can be seven years or more, so this is not a short-term view. Sometimes a strategy will be out of favor for years before it starts to work well and show its value; that doesn't mean your strategy isn't valuable. Just double-check that the theory you have hitched your portfolio to is sound and makes sense for your financial goals.

Which of the following strategies would you most like to explore?

Financial Strategies	**Fitness Strategies**
❏ Modern Portfolio Theory	❏ Spin Classes
❏ Dollar-Cost Averaging	❏ Yoga/Pilates
❏ Active Portfolio Management	❏ High-Intensity Interval Training (HIIT)
❏ Index Funds	❏ Personal Training
	❏ Workout Videos

Listen to Your Body

Your body is smarter than you are. Your mind may think you can be superhuman at times, but your body knows better. In early 2018, I was burning the candle at both ends. I had a teething baby girl, so I wasn't sleeping well at night. I was still trying to wake up early and work out every day. After a while in this routine, I reached a breaking point when work started to get stressful. Although my mind was telling me to work more, sleep less, push harder, my body said, "Nope, I'm giving you shingles." Thankfully, I had a relatively mild case of the virus, but it attacked me and forced me to slow down for several weeks.

You may not get shingles if you push too hard, but your body will respond. You'll get a cold, muscle soreness, or joint pain that will keep you from continuing your hard-driving ways. A person's finances can have the same effect as a screaming, uncomfortable child regarding your sleep. Stress over your money can keep you awake at night, and if you're losing sleep, you're stressing your body. It will eventually respond.

Rest is as vital as work. You will need both work and rest to accomplish your goals. In finance, the equivalent of physical rest could be a brief break from staying so consistent with your budgets after you reach a goal. Maybe you can spend some money on a dinner out because you've surpassed the cash flow goal you had for the week. Don't just keep pushing yourself to pinch and save. It will cause stress and prevent your long-term commitment. In fitness, get enough sleep to let your muscles rest before pushing them again.

> Me - "Dad, it hurts when I go like this."
> Dad - "Don't go like that."

There is some truth in the statement you'll get faster results the harder you work, but that's true only to a point. In swimming, there is a saying that sometimes you have to slow down to go faster. There is a fine line between working hard to see results and pushing too hard, hurting yourself. In health as well as wealth, your body will let you know when you've crossed the line. Listen to your body. If you feel sore, don't work that muscle group today. Take a break. If you're stressing because the budget is a little too tight, loosen up a bit. Your body will tell you what is happening, and if you ignore it, it will let you know... and it will win eventually. This does not mean you abandon your goals or good habits. It means you maintain a reasonable and sustainable balance that spirals in an upward direction, not a downward one.

It can be easy to ignore the signs your body is sending. The straightforward messages to listen to in fitness are soreness and sickness. If you're sore, drink more water, get more rest, and don't work those sore muscles today. They will be better off having a break, and they may benefit from some stretching, yoga, or repetitive low-stress work like walking. When you feel sick, don't try to push through a cold or flu. Your body will not lose your fitness level if you take a few days off, and you'll recover from the illness much faster if you get some rest.

Financial stress and recovery can be a bit more subtle. For many, financial stress shows up in the loss of sleep. Some people can sleep through anything, so if you're one of the lucky few who can sleep through a hurricane, you may have different signs show up when you're stressed about money. Some say the signs they encounter are being distracted at work, a nervous tick such as a twitch in their eye muscles, or picking at their fingernails. Learn yourself and your stress response, so you can listen to the signs you're pushing too hard.

Check-in with yourself periodically to gauge how you're feeling and your stress levels. If you find that your stress levels are regularly high, consider adding a mindfulness practice like meditation to your routine to help regulate that stress and improve your life.

Now is a good time to pan out and revisit the Fit Financial formula:

Mindset + Planning + Habits + Time = Health & Wealth

We've reviewed mindset, planning, and habits. All that's left is time. If you continue your good habits, review them regularly to ensure they are in line with your goals, and keep a positive mindset throughout the process, you will start seeing results in no time. Now you have all the tools, save one – the educational foundation of health and wealth. We will go over the information you need along your journey to a healthy and wealthy life. Once you are armed with the essential knowledge, and you've consistently applied the Pillars of Progress to your life, only time will stand between you and the fitness you dream about in health and wealth.

EDUCATION

Fundamental Truisms

There are two significant problems in today's society concerning health and wealth:
1. The rich are getting richer, while the poor are getting poorer.
2. The fit are getting fitter, while the fat are getting fatter.

According to recent studies, 60-70% of American households will be able to replace 75% of their working income with retirement savings. They will most likely pass away with positive net worth to transition to heirs[6]. Although that number sounds reasonable for society as a whole, the 30-40% of households who are not adequately prepared disagree. By 2030 the CDC estimates 42% of Americans will qualify

---

6 Bajtelsmit, V., & Rappaport, A. (2018). Retirement Adequacy in the United States. *Journal of Financial Service Professionals, 72*(6), 71. https://web-a-ebscohost-com.du.idm.oclc.org/ehost/detail/detail?vid=0&sid=d4ca1a96-c1f1-4948-84e9-28274371b5e0%40sdc-v-sessmgr02&bdata=JnNpdGU9ZWhvc3QtbGl2ZSZzY29wZT1zaXRl#AN=132685640&db=bth

as obese[7]. The habits of basic physical fitness are not being built to support a healthy population. We already see a decrease in health-related quality of life in this country, and declining health will, by definition, continue to decrease this quality of life[8]. The key to solving these problems is education, but there is a difference between being educated and being inundated. This section will provide enough education to send you down the path of measurable success that Americans need to turn the downward spiral of declining fitness into an upward spiral staircase of improvement without overwhelming you with data. Use this information to change your life and share it to help those you care about in changing theirs. Together we can put our whole society on a path to health and wealth fitness.

Money Truisms

Within all the noise and salespeople, you can apply sound theories and practices to manage your financial life. These basic truisms are the foundation of financial planning. Know what they are and how they work before we understand how to construct a fit financial portfolio.

Dollar-Cost Averaging

Dollar-cost averaging is a fancy way to tell people to consistently add a set amount of money to their investment accounts at regular intervals. Over long periods, through dollar-cost averaging your investments, you can purchase shares at an average lower cost than buying larger chunks all at once. This practice of equal amounts at specified intervals works when cashing out as well. Dollar-cost average into an investment as well as dollar-cost average out of an investment, if you can. Dollar-cost aver-

---

[7] CDC Newsroom. (2012, May 7). CDC Weight of the Nation Press Briefing. Retrieved from https://www.cdc.gov/media/releases/2012/t0507_weight_nation.html

[8] Olfson, M., Wall, M., Liu, S., Schoenbaum, M., & Blanco, C. (2018). Declining Health-Related Quality of Life in the U.S. *American Journal of Preventive Medicine,* 54(3), 325-333. https://www-sciencedirect-com.du.idm.oclc.org/science/article/pii/S0749379717307006

aging takes away the need to time the market, as no one really knows what will happen at any given time. If an advisor claims to predict the future, dismiss them as a salesperson, and run away.

Diversification & Asset Allocation

Diversification refers to investing in assets that are not all the same. Buy many different companies across a swath of industries and types of companies. Buy bonds with different time frames. Diversifying your investments will help ensure one foolish mistake by a CEO won't decimate your portfolio. For those who have not heard of it, search "Enron."

Asset allocation is investing in different classes of assets. An asset class is a type of asset like cash, CD's, stocks, bonds, international stocks, etc. Asset allocation was first introduced in Modern Portfolio Theory by Harry Markowitz. He won a Nobel Memorial Prize for the idea that an efficient portfolio, including both stocks and bonds, will provide a greater total return on investment for a given level of risk than a portfolio of either all stocks or all bonds.

Common Question: Where does real estate fit in my portfolio?

Real estate is an alternative investment to stocks and bonds. Rental property can be income-generating as well as a growth asset over time. Real estate is an excellent diversifier, but use it as a part of your overall portfolio and not as the entire portfolio for the same reason you would not use stocks for your entire portfolio. If the real estate market crumbles, you want to make sure your assets are diversified. Also, beware of over-leveraging your real estate investments by using too much debt to buy the properties. When managing investment properties, a good rule is:

do not have more mortgage payments required than you could cover with your own cash flow, should you lose a renter. This way, if you cannot find another renter for an extended time, you can still maintain the debt obligation without losing your investment to foreclosure.

Many believe they are either a real estate person or a stock person. The fact is, you would benefit from being both. Whether you invest in actual properties or investment vehicles that manage the properties for you, like real estate investment trusts (REITs), having real estate in your portfolio to diversify beyond the stock and bond market is a good idea.

There is a small but distinct difference between diversification and asset allocation: diversification refers to buying multiple securities within an asset class, whereas asset allocation refers to buying securities in a swath of asset classes like large-cap, small-cap, bonds, international, etc. A balanced portfolio, both diversified and appropriately allocated, will smooth out your ride and provide a better return for an overall lower risk through full market cycles.

Inflation

Inflation is the killer of retirements. To keep the concept as basic as possible, inflation is the increasing cost of goods: milk, gas, electricity, clothes, bananas, etc. As these goods get more expensive, the ability your dollar has to buy them goes down. A one-dollar soda today will be a dollar fifty in a few years. If all you have is that same dollar because it's been saved in a safe somewhere, you won't have enough to buy a soda. If someone retires and withdraws all of their money out of growth investments and into cash to reduce their risk exposure, they are actually increasing their risk. Inflation will eat away at the value of their cash, guaranteeing a loss of purchasing power. Yes, they assure their actual account value stays the same, but that account value won't buy the same amount of goods and services tomorrow it can today. In the chart below, you can see the cost of a soda rising over 20 years:

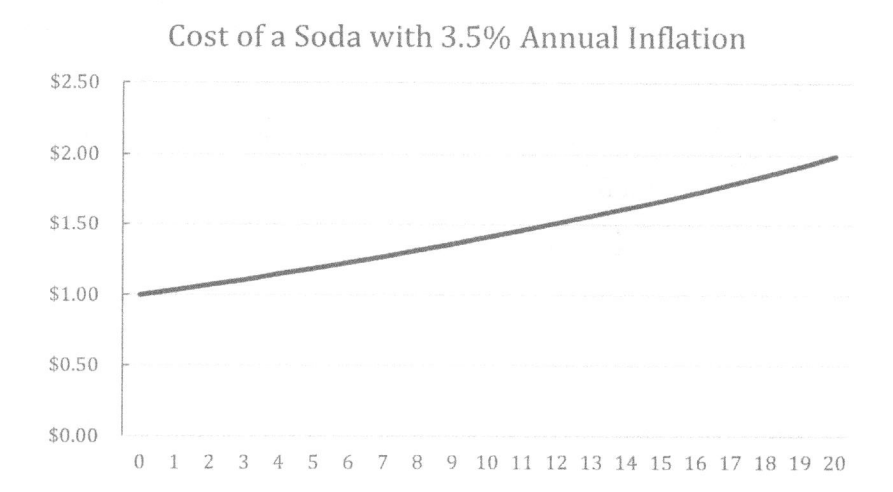

Cost of a Soda with 3.5% Annual Inflation

Compound Interest

Albert Einstein is credited in having said, "Compound interest is the eighth wonder of the world. He who understands it earns it. He who doesn't pays it." Interest is the amount of money you earn on an investment. **Compound interest** is the interest you can earn on the investment *plus* interest on the previous interest you've earned. Compound interest is what people are referencing when they say their money works for them. This interest growth doesn't seem like a big deal when looking at a short time, but finance is a long-term game. When you evaluate compound interest over long periods, the growth on your growth can make a considerable positive difference if you're participating. If you're investing with compound interest over a long period of time, you'll have a much higher account value than without it. On the other hand, if you're paying a loan with compound interest, you will pay far more for that loan over time than you would with simple interest. Here are two examples:

Positive Compound Interest
To earn $1,000,000 with a 7% compounded interest rate, you'd have to invest the following amounts depending on the amount of time you have to reach that goal:

10 years	$5,777.51 per month	$693,301.20 total investment
20 years	$1,919.66	$460,718.40
30 years	$ 819.69	$294,728.40*

*Notice if you have 3x the amount of time, you can invest *7x less* per month, and you'll invest *less than 50%* of the total amount of funds in reaching the same million-dollar amount at the end of the different investment periods.

Negative Compound Interest
To pay off a $250,000 mortgage at a 5% interest:

| 30-year mortgage | $1,342.05 per month | $233,139.44 total interest paid |
| 15-year mortgage | $1,976.98 | $105,857.13* |

For 30% more monthly loan payment, you save 50% of the interest and half the time.

A decision in financial planning is only partially math. Many other factors go into what choice to make for yourself, so please only take these calculations as a way to understand compound interest, not as a recommendation of what to do for your individualized future.

Heath Truisms

There are two specific health principles to point out: 1. weight is not an essential measurement for success, and 2. the law of thermodynamics is the only law you need to follow to increase or decrease your overall weight. The science is sound and straightforward, and salespeople will often overcomplicate how weight works in the human body to sell their books, products, or exercise solutions. Don't fall for these traps and keep the straightforward science in mind.

Weight

Weight is not a measure of success or failure on its own. What is the preferred metric for your health? How you feel and how you look. What does either of those have to do with how much you weigh? Nothing. Weight is defined as the amount of force an object applies to the ground. In physics, force is equal to mass times acceleration, and in the case of weight, the acceleration is gravity. Mass comprises many things: fat, muscle, bones, internal organs, skin, water, etc. Therefore, weight is a function of the force you apply to the ground-based on the amount of fat and all the other physical components your body has.

It's concerning when someone says, "I just need to lose 10 lbs." The focus on weight proves science is losing the battle against marketing, and the weight loss companies are making a pretty penny on the confusion. Maybe they actually need to stay the same weight but add some muscle to their mix. Sure, maybe they do need to lose fat—many people do—but call a spade a spade. They need to lose fat, not weight. If you watch those World's Strongest Man competitions, you'll see those men are morbidly obese based on height and weight alone. They are also not as unhealthy as their numbers would imply because their body fat percentages are typically in a healthy range. As a stand-alone measurement, weight is a meaningless assessment of health. So, you can stop worrying about your weight alone.

> **Common Misconception: How can I lose the fat on my...?**
>
> Too many articles talk about how you can "lose stubborn belly fat with these three simple exercises." Don't read that article, please. That's the only way we can get the click-bait to go away. You, unfortunately, cannot remove fat from your body in one place and not another. If you have a chicken arm, a spare tire, thunder thighs, a double chin, or any other place you'd love to lose fat, you'll have to lose fat all over to get rid of it. Genetics and body type determine where someone stores their fat, and I'm sorry to say it's almost guaranteed the most hated fat on your body will be the last to go away. That's not backed by science, just experience.
>
> Stick with the basic principles for eating less than you burn, and you'll see progress. If you put in the effort it takes for all-around, long-term health, you could lose the most stubborn fat stores and hopefully never find them again.

Unfortunately, the health gurus' preaching will tell you how to lose "weight" with their meal plans and products. Weight loss alone is not an appropriate goal. A focus on weight loss can become discouraging because many people gain weight when they start a workout program. When you first get started, you will most likely gain muscle quickly if you haven't worked out in a long time. This will make the scale read a higher number even though that muscle is good for you; muscle is denser than fat, so you will have more weight in a smaller space. Muscle also helps your body burn more calories while at rest because the muscle needs to use energy to maintain itself. Burning more calories at rest can then lead to positive weight loss over time through thermodynamics, as described next. Many new to exercise have been discouraged by the short-term weight gain even when other, favored metrics are improving.

That discouragement can lead to someone quitting a new regimen that was quite beneficial.

To start, put the scale away. Let your body do its thing. Weigh yourself only when you take the rest of your measurements to keep your weight in perspective and evaluate its significance as part of a complete health profile. Most people will gain weight while losing inches all over their bodies when beginning an exercise regimen. People want to lose inches, not weight. Losing weight is just the vernacular used, and it is confusing for those who don't know what it really means. Don't get discouraged so early in the journey.

The Law of Thermodynamics

The law of thermodynamics is a physics concept regarding heat and the use of energy. When applied to the body, thermodynamics is the relationship between the intake of calories through food and the body's caloric expenditure to complete functions like beating the heart and moving in general. A calorie is merely a unit of measure for energy. When you determine a sandwich has 550 calories, you are calculating the amount of energy the sandwich provides the person who eats it. If you have a surplus of energy, it is stored in the body as fat and kept for later use. If there is a deficit of energy, the body will pull from its stores to generate the needed supply. Therefore, if you want to lose fat and inches on your body, part of the work comes in the form of exercise, but most of your results will be found with food. It's a lot easier not to eat 200 calories than to burn 200 calories.

The law of thermodynamics is real and applies to our bodies no matter what gimmicky marketers have to say. If you eat more calories than you burn, you'll gain weight. If you eat fewer calories than you burn, you'll lose weight. I used the term "weight" here on purpose. The type of food you're eating or not eating will determine what type of weight you lose or gain. If your diet consists of mostly saturated fats and refined sugars—even though you're eating fewer calories than you're burning—you will lose muscle, not fat. If you eat a proper balance of macronutrients while maintaining an appropriate resistance training routine, you will gain muscle, not fat.

Proper caloric intake is covered further in the next section. For now, just remember your overall relationship between caloric intake and expense is the most important dynamic for your overall body composition.

These basic principles of health and wealth lay the foundation for an in-depth look at the parallels between the two aspects of our lives. The next several sections will provide further information that illustrates the similarities. The first of those sections will cover cash and calorie flow. Money in, money out, calories eaten, calories burned.

Summary Takeaways

- Dollar-Cost Averaging – consistent investment means less cost on average over.
- Diversification – spread the risk around, so one problem doesn't shrink a portfolio.
- Asset Allocation – using different types of assets can capitalize on multiple opportunities.
- Inflation – costs of the same items typically increase over time.
- Compound Interest – the most powerful asset you have is time.
- Weight – not an independent measure of health.
- Thermodynamics – eat more calories than you burn: gain weight; eat less than you burn: lose weight.

Cash & Calorie Flow

The most foundational aspect of someone's health and wealth is their flow. By flow, I mean cash flow in finances and calorie flow in fitness. Your cash and your calories alone cannot build the fitness you'd like in either health or wealth, but they are the building blocks. Most people cannot save enough to reach their goals, even with the best investments in the world, if they don't manage their cash flow. Similarly, most people cannot get down to the bodyfat percentage they've always needed to reach their goal, regardless of how great their metabolism, without a handle on their calories.

Having a handle on your flow is not scary, not a lot of work. Like any change in life, initially, it will take some effort, but it gets easy real fast. If you can create your habits based on these foundational elements of your fitness in both aspects, you will have the fundamentals to create the life you want.

Cash Flow

Do you know why some people are in good financial shape, and most are not? Those in good shape pay attention to their cash outflows for both needs and wants. Monitoring your cash flow to ensure it matches your priorities is where the magic happens. If you skipped over the earlier section about finding your priorities, now would be the time to go back to the Planning Pillar of Progress or the Priorities Worksheet and define your priorities. I'll wait here...take your time.

So now that you've actually completed the priorities exercise, you can work on your cash flow. Our society often uses the terms cash flow and budgeting interchangeably; however, they have different meanings. Cash flow is the amount of money flowing in and out of a business or personal cash position. Budgeting is a restriction of the amount of cash flow applied to a particular area of your expenses. The typical relationship we have with budgeting is all about cutting costs, and the reason it doesn't feel good is the impression you are restricted in having what you want (exactly like dieting for calories). The real intention of cash flow monitoring is not to restrict the things you love but to cut the costs you don't care about so much, so we can keep the expenses you prioritize. Once you know you're only cutting out items you don't value, budgeting becomes much more comfortable and, for some, quite fun. If you don't find this fun, find someone who does and let their enthusiasm infect you as they support you in going through the process. You could elicit a professional financial coach or just a friend who cares about your finances. Your AccountabiliBuddy can come in real handy with these tough tasks.

Even if you're already rolling in dough, saving what you need to hit all your goals, and making more money than you can spend, still keep an eye on your cash flow. Not to save even more money than you need for your goals, but because you don't need to squander your hard-earned money on things you don't care about. Spend money on what *you* want. Americans often make the mistake of buying shiny objects and toys just because they think they *should* want them. Just because you make good money doesn't mean you have to want a fancy car. If you authentically do want one and can afford it, fine. But, if you don't care about a luxury item, put your resources to work somewhere else in your life: a charity you'd like to support, kids or grandkids to whom you'd like to gift money, or even for random acts of kindness. Whatever you care about, apply your free cash flow to those expenses. Don't waste your resources.

Monitoring Your Cash Flow

There are a few different ways to monitor your expenses. You could use an online tool like mint.com. As long as you're willing to put up with ads for credit cards and other savings accounts, it's a free app and website. There are other options out there, and some of those come with a fee and no ads. Once you link all your income and spending accounts, programs like this will automatically track where you spend your funds. At first, you'll have to teach the program a few things. For instance, Trader Joe's is a grocery expense, not a convenience store purchase.

You may need to create some categories as well. You can decide how precisely to track your spending at big box vendors like Target or Wal-Mart, where you can buy groceries, furniture, and electronics all in one trip. I've had clients who stopped shopping at stores like this for groceries and instead go to King Soopers or Kroger, so they can have more accurately tracked expenses for a category they care about. You can also use a 'miscellaneous' category for those big box stores, but some like to itemize their expenses into more specific groupings. I've also had clients who stop using certain credit or bank cards because their institution isn't affiliated and doesn't link into their tracker of choice. Is it easier to change a credit card than an expense tracker?

You could also track your expenses in an old-fashioned way. Gather the last three to six months of credit card, bank, or other expense statements and compile your cash flow numbers by hand or on a spreadsheet. A few months of information will give you an idea of where your funds go, and then you can compare your expenses with the priorities outlined. Do they match? For most people, the answer is no. If not, what habits can you shift to align your outflows more closely with your priorities? Almost everyone will find excess resources they didn't know they had. Now it's time to put those resources to work. But how?

Common Question: What percentage do I pay in taxes on the money I make?

2019 Income Tax Rate Table:

Income Tax Rate	Single	Married, filing jointly	Married, filing separately	Head of Household
10%	$0 to 9,700	$0 to $19,400	$0 to 9,700	$0 to 13,850
12%	$9,701 to 39,475	$19,401 to 78,950	$9,701 to 39,475	$13,851 to 52,850

22%	$39,476 to 84,200	$78,951 to 168,400	$39,476 to 84,200	$52,851 to 84,200
24%	$84,201 to 160,725	$168,401 to 321,450	$84,201 to 160,725	$84,201 to 160,700
32%	$160,726 to 204,100	$321,451 to 408,200	$160,726 to 204,100	$160,701 to 204,100
35%	$204,101 to 510,300	$408,201 to 612,350	$204,101 to 306,175	$204,101 to 510,300
37%	$510,301 or more	$612,351 or more	$306,176 or more	$510,301 or more

Income taxes are often misunderstood. Most people think they pay the rate at which their income falls on the IRS table published every year. The tax rates from those charts start relatively low at 10% in 2019 and increase in percentage as you make more money and reach higher income thresholds, up to 37% on the highest earners. There is a common misconception people with higher tax rates pay a higher rate on *all* of their income. This is not true. You only pay the higher tax rate on the income above a certain threshold (see the table above). That means if your income moves you into the higher rate by $10, you'll pay the higher tax rate on only $10 of income. The rest of your income is taxed at the appropriate levels. Your highest tax rate, or the one on the table that corresponds with your adjusted gross income, is referred to as your marginal tax rate.

Once you have calculated all of your annual income and the actual taxes you owe for the year, you can determine the more relevant number: your effective tax rate. **The effective tax rate** is the total rate at which you are actually paying taxes.

Taxes can be confusing when all is said and done. Look on the first few pages of your prepared tax return and find your adjusted gross income as well as your total taxes owed. Divide the total taxes owed by your gross income. This is your effective tax rate or the rate you actually paid to Uncle Sam last year.

$$\frac{Amount\ of\ Total\ Taxes\ Owed}{Total\ Gross\ Income} = Effective\ Tax\ Rate$$

The Goldfish Effect

Whether you get a raise at work or you save money and prioritize your expenses, you will have an increase of cash flow, and you'll need to have a plan for the newfound funds, or as everyone else does, you'll spend those resources without giving them a second thought. This is the goldfish effect. As a goldfish tank gets bigger, the fish get bigger. As a typical person's income increases, their expenses increase with it. Don't be that cliché. When you have an increase in income or a decrease in expenses, know what you're going to do with the difference. The steps to take with your newfound cashflows are:

1. High-interest debt
2. Emergency funds
3. Retirement
4. Low-interest debt or savings goals

Let's dig a little deeper:

Paying Down Debt

High-interest debt can be a headwind on the journey to financial freedom. The typical example of high-interest debt is credit cards with interest rates at 12% or higher. In exchange for the bank giving you the ability to buy that experience or item before you have the cash to pay for it, you will overpay for that item in the form of a bank service fee called interest. Having a regular payment for something you purchased a long time ago will restrict your future ability to use the cash flow you have. For the typical American, it will lead to further borrowing to buy the lifestyle you want. The high-interest debt trap is a vicious downward spiral.

Other debts with much lower interest rates can benefit your financial plan if used appropriately, but we will cover those a bit later.

When you have increased your overall cash flow through either a raise, promotion, or prioritized cash flow, start paying down your high-interest debt first. High interest is any rate higher than a typical federal student loan. (You can look the student loan rates up on the web, but they change regularly and are a pretty good measure of what constitutes high interest at any given time. At the time of writing, they are somewhere between 5-7%.) If you have credit card debt that stays on the card for more than a month, you're not paying the list price for anything you buy. You're paying far more than that price due to the interest that's accruing every day. If you are loaded with 12-20+% interest credit cards, it doesn't make a lot of mathematical sense to put money in a savings account, paying you less than 2%. One month of interest gain on $1,000 at a 2% annual savings account rate is $1.67, whereas the credit card interest at 12% in one month would be $10. That's a big difference for one month, and the difference compounds quickly over months and into years. Pay these high debt loans off as quickly as possible.

For now, rank your debt from the highest interest rate to the lowest rate still above the federal student loan rates. Pay the minimum payment on every one of the debts besides the top one. Put all other resources to pay down the debt until it is gone. Then move to the next on the list keeping the total dollar amount going to pay down debt the same. Keep repeating this process until all these debts are knocked out. If you'd like help, use the debt tool on the fitfinancialapproach.com website.

If an emergency comes up while you are paying down debt, you may need to use the room you've created on the credit cards in order to cover the emergency. An emergency does not mean a sale at your local t-shirt store. It is a legitimate emergency you may need to dip into funds to cover. If there's a way to postpone the purchase—even if you have to remain slightly uncomfortable for a time to not add debt to your high-interest cards—pick that option. For example, if riding your bike to work for a while is an option and allows you to delay buying new tires for your car, do that instead. You'll be thankful later, and you'll get some bonus health benefits.

Your low-interest debt—student loans, car loans with reasonable rates, mortgages—can wait for the moment. We will get to those later. Set up your emergency fund next.

Common Question: How much am I actually paying for something I put on a credit card?

For the sake of this example, let's say your credit card comes with a 14% annual interest rate that accrues monthly—many accrue daily, which leads to an even higher amount of interest. If you buy a $2,000 vacation on that card and pay $150 per month until it's paid off, which is typically more than the minimum, it would take you over 14 months to pay off the debt and cost you a total of nearly $175 in interest. Most people pay closer to the minimums, so the effects of high-interest debt are even worse. Let's say the minimum on this card was $35. It would take 95 months to pay it off and cost $1,315 in total interest. On top of the higher interest cost, you had probably booked another trip before the first trip was paid off and overpaid for the next one as well.

Setting Up Emergency Funds

Eventually, an emergency fund should have three to six months' worth of your non-discretionary expenses in accessible cash. Non-discretionary expenses are the "have to" costs. Most of these "have to" expenses are straightforward, like your mortgage, utilities, and necessary loan payments. Some are not so cut and dry. The best way to know which expenses are non-discretionary is to imagine you just lost your income entirely. Decide what you are going to continue to pay for and what you are going to cut? Whatever you would continue paying would be considered a "have to" expense. Add all those costs up for one month and multiply by three. That's the minimum amount you'll want to carry in your emergency fund at any given time.

For couples where both partners contribute to the household cash flow at somewhat equal levels, and both have low chances of losing their income, three months of emergency funds are enough. For instance, in my household, we keep about a three-month emergency fund because we both contribute to our household income, are in different industries, and the likelihood of losing our income at the same time is relatively low. If, however, only one spouse is bringing in income (staying at home is an exceedingly noble profession), or one of the two incomes has a higher likelihood of decreasing in the future, set aside six months' of your non-discretionary expenses. The higher your risk, the more you need to have saved for emergencies.

Don't overfund your emergency reserves. Your emergency fund will be invested in cash, which will not earn a level of interest that keeps up with inflation over time. Those funds held in cash will be losing buying power while keeping the funds out of your investment plan. If you have too much in your cash account, you are hurting your overall financial plan.

With your cash savings, you do not need to feel guilty using your emergency reserves. People with fully-funded emergency funds will put their new furnace on a credit card because they didn't want their savings to dip below the recommended level. What on earth? That's precisely what it's there for. It's okay to use your emergency funds, then revert additional funds from your savings as long as you need to build back your emergency reserves.

Start by saving the minimum level of three months of non-discretionary expenses in your emergency fund. Once you reach the three-month level, advance to the next step and fund your retirement. After your retirement is on track, you can come back to round out your emergency funds and build up to the six-month level later, if your situation justifies it.

Planning for Retirement

Once you have the minimum saved for unexpected emergencies, you can start setting aside a portion of your earnings for retirement. The ideal percentage of your gross income to save for retirement is 10-20%, depending on how close you are to retirement when you start saving. The closer you are to retiring, the higher percentage to set aside. For now, understand your retirement plan and their matching structures—many plans through employers will match your contributions to give you an incentive to use the plan. You can get this information from your HR department or reach out to the company that sponsors your plan. When just getting started, at least take advantage of your company's match. That match is the equivalent of getting an immediate return on your investment and adding it immediately to your retirement plan. If your company doesn't have a matching plan or even a retirement plan at all, you can use other vehicles to invest for your future. Some of these vehicles are covered in the next chapter. Even if quitting work is not your future goal, use long-term retirement vehicles to take advantage of the tax benefits, and provide yourself with future options. Many people don't have the financial freedom to choose the day they retire; the date is chosen for them due to being laid off or physically unable to do the job. Start saving early, as time is your most valuable resource.

Common Question: Should I pay off my home or invest the money?

It totally depends. Is retirement just around the corner, or do you have a long time to save? Are you relocating soon or staying in this property for a while? How high is your interest rate? All kinds of questions go into this equation of 'pay off home vs. invest money,' but here are a few **reasons to pay it off.**

- ❏ If you're in the final stages of work-life and trying to pare down your expenses to prepare for the loss of income in retirement, by all means, pay off your home.
- ❏ If you're in a precarious position at work or in an industry where you think your income could drastically change for the worse in the future, you may want to pay off your obligations to lessen the burden if your income is lost.
- ❏ If you have to pay mortgage insurance, you may want to reduce your loan to an appropriate level of equity vs. debt, so you can remove the insurance or refinance into a mortgage that does not have the added expense. Typically, you need to own at least 20% of your home's value to refinance without mortgage insurance.

There are also several **situations where you wouldn't want to pay it off**.

- ❏ If you're able to invest the funds and earn more than you're paying in mortgage interest after taxes, then you would be mathematically better off investing your money. Not only could you beat the interest charged to you, but you might also have more flexibility with those funds.

❑ If you have all your assets tied up in your home, an illiquid asset, it can be difficult to get your money out if you need access for any reason. If your assets are in an accessible investment and a situation arises where you'd be better off without the loan, you could use the flexibility of a liquid investment to cash out and pay off your home. Flexibility doesn't always make you money, but it does add to your financial planning agility.

Saving for Goals

There's a decision to make at this point, and the correct answer depends on your stage in life. Do you pay down your lower interest debt first or save for mid-term goals? Either one could be the right place to start, but you'll want to tackle both eventually. If you're going to put your next family trip on a credit card or steal from your emergency fund to pay for the vacay, then you need to start saving for the vacation first. If you don't have any big expenses coming up to speak of, other than the unexpected emergencies you've already saved for, now is the time to pay off those loans. (Other than your mortgage.) Rank the debts from highest interest to lowest and get to work the same way as before.

Once the smaller interest rate debts are paid off, you can ramp up all your savings. If you have reached this point, you are in the upper echelon of wealth-building Americans. Not many people can say a mortgage is their only debt, *and* they have a fully-funded emergency fund. Congratulations, now it's time to manifest your true wealth. With your debts paid off, you can now redirect the loan payment amount to your retirement plans and mid-term goals. The amounts to add to retirement vs. mid-term goals will be dependent upon your individual goals and ability to save. If you have a comfortable current lifestyle, and all your future goals are appropriately funded, you can continue saving for unknown future goals as they will inevitably arise. Use liquid investments for savings not tied to a specific goal as you never know when the goal will become apparent, and the investment vehicle for that specific goal needs to change. Your continued savings add to your pool, allowing options later in life as your priorities change. Make sure to adjust your savings amounts as needed by increasing or decreasing your monthly contribution. If you get a raise, save a portion of that raise. If you have an upcoming expense, add less to your investments for a while to cover it. With three kids, I knew we would take at least one trip to Disney World in Orlando. We started saving for it when my first-born was little, and because we started so early, we will be able to stay on property, purchase VIP passes, meal plans, the works. We may even be able to pay for grandparents to come along and help out. If you start early, a little bit can go a long way.

Cash flow is the foundation of wealth. To reach your goals for wealth, you'll need to get your cash flow under control. The work you put in upfront will pay off once you start to see the results. Once you've taken a few steps in the process, it becomes fun for even the most skeptical. Fun might seem like a stretch now, but you'll enjoy the process more as your cash flow improves. No matter what area of your life is changing for the better, personal growth is always fun once you get past the first few hurdles.

Calorie Flow

Eat less than you burn to lose weight. Eat more than you burn to gain. This statement is a simplification of thermodynamics in the body. Food is fuel. Your body uses fuel to run its most basic functions, like breathing and beating your heart. It also uses fuel to complete tasks like running, jumping, and even sitting on the couch. The body isn't like a car, however. If your car runs out of gas, you're on the side of the road, not moving again until you fill the tank. If you don't fuel your body with good food, your body will go to the stores of energy it has socked away for safekeeping. All day, you are burning energy.

The human body adapted to life as a hunter-gatherer by storing the extra energy from the food we ate to sustain ourselves while searching for our next meal, even if it took a few days. In today's world, we don't have to go days, or even hours, without food as there are opportunities to eat everywhere. Advances in modern technology allow for mass production, processing, and food delivery to the developed world; we collectively have more access to food than we have ever had as a species. The easy access to food solved a problem humanity has had for millennia while creating an entirely new problem: overeating. We still store energy for a period of deprivation and starvation that doesn't regularly occur in modern-day, developed countries. Your body fat is supposed to be your emergency fund, but just like your cash emergency fund, having too much is just as ill-advised as having too little.

We have a few ways to measure our food intake to ensure we are not overeating, but even those methods can be misinterpreted and confusing. The daily recommended values printed on the food labels are the caloric recommendation for a 150-pound man. Unless you just happen to be that guy, you'll need to adjust the values for your weight. If you're a 130-pound woman, 2,000 calories a day is probably too much for you. If you're a bigger guy, 2,000 calories would feel like starving yourself. Everyone is different, and everyone has different goals. The starting place is finding your **average daily burn rate**; given your current size, body type, and typical activity levels throughout the day, you can estimate your calorie needs to maintain your weight.

The following are the formulas to determine your base daily burn rate at rest:

❏ Men
Daily Burn = 88.362 + 13.397*Weight in kg + 4.799*Height in cm − 5.667*Age in years

❏ Women
Daily Burn = 447.593 + 9.247*Weight in kg + 3.098*Height in cm − 4.330*Age in years

Use a converter to change your weight from pounds to kilograms and your height from feet and inches to centimeters. Once you have your daily number of calories you burn when you don't leave the couch, you have to adjust for your activity level. That adjustment is made using the activity multiplier:

Exercise Level	Description	Activity Multiplier
Little to no exercise	Sedentary lifestyle	Base rate x 1.2
Light exercise	Exercise 1-3 times a week	Base rate x 1.375
Moderate exercise	Exercise 3-5 times a week	Base rate x 1.55
Heavy exercise	Exercise 6-7 times a week	Base rate x 1.725

Don't feel too tied to what the results tell you. They are more of a guide. You may find you are losing weight too quickly or not losing weight at all while sticking to your target. You may find you're too hungry throughout the day to maintain a certain calorie intake goal for more than a few days. Give yourself permission for trial and error until you find the right caloric intake level for you.

If your goal is **losing weight**, take the estimated daily burn rate, subtract a couple of hundred calories, and count your food intake to make sure you stay under your daily target to see a change over time. It is not healthy to lose more than two pounds a week, so don't restrict your diet too much at any given time. At more than two pounds per week, you run the risk of losing muscle as well as fat, and maintaining muscle can help you burn even more fat. More to come on that in the next section. Restricting your caloric intake too much also makes the fat loss process difficult to maintain and defeats the purpose of creating a sustainable lifestyle. A more modest restriction of calories is a lifestyle and will take a while to get where you want to be. Just make more healthy choices than unhealthy ones over time, and you will get there. As noted before, keep your long-term goals in mind when determining your daily routines, and develop a plan you can stick to until your goals change. Once you've reached your goal weight and fat percentage or found a healthy point where you'd like to stay, adjust the daily calorie intake goal to maintenance rather than weight loss.

If you're one of those trying **to gain weight,** you need to eat more than your typical burn rate. I was one of these people while a personal trainer. My clients hated to hear me complain about how much I had to eat, but it was the truth. Eating more on purpose when you're not hungry feels just as uncomfortable as not eating when your brain tells you that you are hungry. The grass is always greener, right? If you're looking for muscle gains, they take time. On average, you can gain about half a pound a week if you're trying to add muscle without adding too much body fat. There is no way to naturally bulk up quickly without adding both muscle and fat at the same time. While in a heavy resistance training phase, you may want to increase your protein consumption to repair the muscle you're breaking down in the gym. I'll get into this in a bit more detail in the next chapter.

Common Misconception: Supplements are key to reaching my fitness goals

The weight loss and workout supplement industry has exploded in the past few decades. It is now a multiple billion-dollar industry, and the funny thing is few supplements have been tested to do what they say they do for the human body. All supplements have printed somewhere on their packaging, "these claims have not been verified by the Food and Drug Administration." So long as the companies don't claim to cure an illness or disease, supplement makers can allege whatever they want. Outrageous.

Caffeine—a thermogenic and diuretic supplement that supports weight loss—is one of the most researched supplements out there. Many studies have confirmed caffeine helps people lose weight in the short term, but the type of weight is not what most people are looking for. The thermogenic aspect of caffeine increases your heart rate to a level that helps burn calories. The diuretic part makes you urinate more, which leads to less water retained by the body. In the short term, both of these reactions will support weight loss. However, currently, there is no definitive evidence caffeine will help you lose weight over long periods, nor keep the weight off. Please, don't waste your money on a weight loss supplement loaded with caffeine. They claim their powder will help you lose weight just because caffeine is an ingredient in the mix, and they add sugar or salt to make it taste better while those ingredients are working against the weight loss benefits. Psychologists have also determined that, for most people, taking a weight loss supplement will lead them to eat more unhealthy food and drink sugary drinks the rest of the day because they think the supplement is doing all the work[9]. This laissez-faire approach completely defeats the purpose, especially when the weight loss benefits from the supplements aren't long term. Unhealthy eating will be hard to overcome long term. The more straightforward and more practical answer is: save your money and make healthier food choices.

---

9   Chang, Yevvon Yi-Chi, and Wen-Bin Chiou. "Taking Weight-loss Supplements May Elicit Liberation from Dietary Control. A Laboratory Experiment." *Appetite* 72.C (2014): 8-12. Web.

Another highly researched supplement is **creatine**. Taking creatine will help your body recover faster from hard workouts and retain water. The water retention caused by creatine will make your muscles look larger than they really are in the short term, and the recovery will help your strength and performance. They have found no long-term side effects if the doses you take are reasonable with an appropriate amount of water intake. The recommended amount of creatine to take is .03g/kg of body weight/day. They have found a few side effects from creatine when inappropriately used. In the summary of creatine, "when taken without sufficient water, stomach cramping can occur. Diarrhea and nausea can occur when too much creatine is taken at once, in which doses should be spread out throughout the day and taken with meals"[10] The recovery and water retention benefits with low risk of side effects sound great on the surface. The truth is you have to be training heavily to realize the benefits of creatine. Even if you're lifting weights, you have to lift hard to break down your muscles enough to need something like creatine to recover. If you're not pushing your limits in muscle-building activities and breaking down your body, that protein shake with the other ingredients difficult to pronounce is really just added calories to your day. So, put your money toward your cash flow priorities instead, drink more water and get more sleep.

Although the FDA does not verify claims made by vitamin and supplement companies, some groups perform scientific, third-party studies of supplements to see if enough quality research has been done to substantiate the claims. If you take the time to evaluate the actual research performed on these vitamins, you'll see there isn't much to the claims being made. If you're taking a multi-vitamin, fish oil omega-3, iron, or any other vitamin without a medical profes-

---

[10] https://examine.com/supplements/creatine/#summary13, accessed 12/18/2019

sional's recommendation, look at the studies behind the marketing assertions. You're probably wasting your money.

If you're still sore a few days after your workout sessions, and you're finding it hard to move without pain, you may be a good candidate for supplements in the short term, just to get you going. Once you're in the normal range of sore for a day after a hard workout and you're able to move around without pain on day two, you most likely don't need them anymore. The difference between a good workout sore and a bad workout sore is the ability to still complete the motions you're asking of your body even though it hurts. If you're too sore to wash your hair, you're too sore. If while washing your hair, your arms and shoulders feel a little tight, that's okay.

For the regular fitness enthusiast who is not trying to become a fitness model or bodybuilder, you're throwing your money away buying supplements. Recovery is covered more in the quick fixes section, but the basics are to eat better, sleep more, and drink more water. Then you can take the money you would be using on supplements to invest in your emergency funds, which will have you sleeping even better at night, and the positive upward spiral of fitness and wealth can begin.

A Balanced Diet

The general advice for the masses is to eat a balanced diet, but what does that mean? If you were paying attention in the '80s and '90s, you'd remember the government came out with the food pyramid in an attempt to explain what a balanced diet looks like. Recently, the food pyramid changed. Who knew? The current food pyramid looks different, but it is still too confusing to remember. How much is in a serving? We're supposed to remember the six different food groups and how much of each to eat at varying levels every day? We need something easier to follow. Take a look:

The old food pyramid:

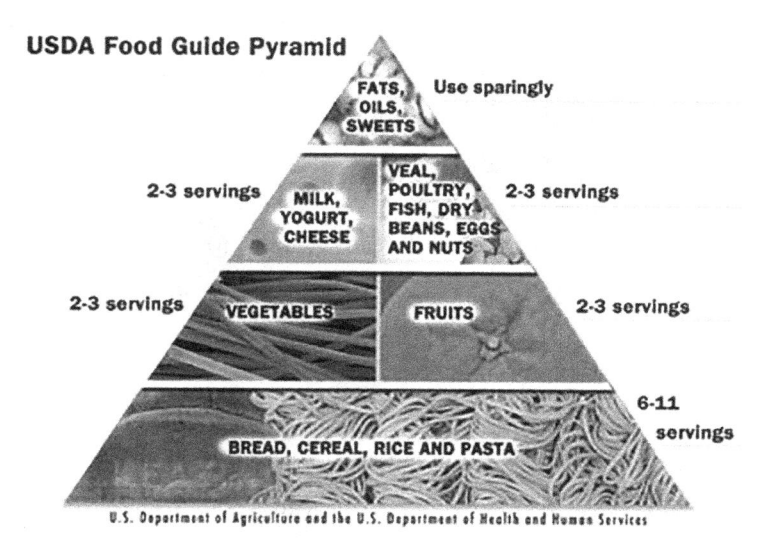

USDA Food Guide Pyramid

- FATS, OILS, SWEETS — Use sparingly
- MILK, YOGURT, CHEESE — 2-3 servings
- VEAL, POULTRY, FISH, DRY BEANS, EGGS AND NUTS — 2-3 servings
- VEGETABLES — 2-3 servings
- FRUITS — 2-3 servings
- BREAD, CEREAL, RICE AND PASTA — 6-11 servings

U.S. Department of Agriculture and the U.S. Department of Health and Human Services

The newer food pyramid (This seems less confusing?):

MyPyramid
STEPS TO A HEALTHIER YOU
MyPyramid.gov

GRAINS | VEGETABLES | FRUITS | MILK | MEAT & BEANS

A balanced diet is composed of all the macronutrients, carbohydrates, protein, and fat. Everything you eat consists of at least one of these three macros, and much of what humans eat consists of multiple macronutrients. The point of a balanced diet is that every macronutrient serves a purpose and belongs in your diet.

Carbohydrates provide short-term energy to help with the normal day-to-day functions like walking, lifting your groceries out of the car, and basically any movement you make.

- **Protein** is the building block of the body. All those bodily movements you make every day—even without lifting weights—break down your muscles, and protein is used to repair those breakdowns and improve the body for the next time you might do whatever it is you did to break it down.

- **Fat** is a horribly named macronutrient as it is not at all like fat on the body. The scientific name for this macronutrient is **lipid**. Why do lipids have a nickname? Is the word lipid much more difficult to understand than carbohydrate? Anyway, fats support brain functions and lubricate our joints. This is *not* a bad thing. A long time ago, it was thought too much fat in a diet led to our bodies adding more fat and, consequently, heart disease. Clearly, this belief is erroneous as the movement to reduce the fat in our diet shot society's bodyfat level through the roof when sugar was added to the foods to improve their taste. Lipids also help with satiety, or the feeling of being full, which tells your brain to stop eating. We could definitely use more of that as a society–the stopping part–as the worldwide prevalence of obesity has doubled since the 1980s.[11]

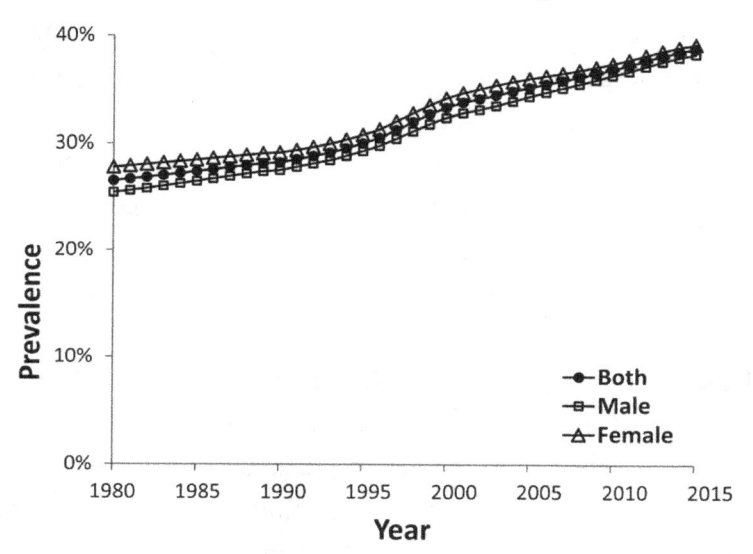

Global trends in overweight

Global trends in obesity

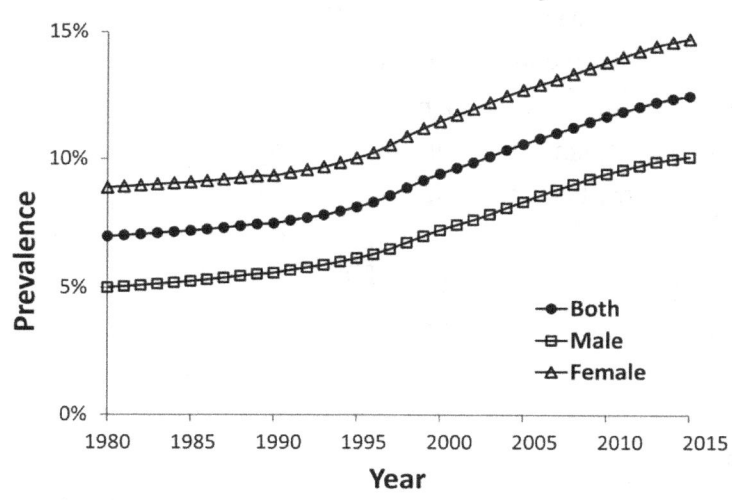

---

11   Chooi, Y. C., Ding, C., & Magkos, F. (2019). The epidemiology of obesity. *Metabolism, 92*, 6-10.

The percentage of each macronutrient in your overall caloric intake will vary depending on your body type, activity levels, and long-term goals. Suppose your workout routine consists mainly of endurance cardio like running or swimming long distances. In that case, your intake may consist of a higher percentage of carbohydrates than someone doing more yoga or another less aerobic form of exercise. Instead of researching all the different options and choices you have concerning how much of your diet consists of each macronutrient, go to an online calculator to determine an appropriate starting breakdown of macronutrient percentages for your diet. There are resources on the fitfinancialapproach.com website. Once you have the starting place, see how the shift in calorie intake feels and how your body reacts to the new breakdown of macros. If you need to adjust, use trial and error to figure out the right percentage breakdown for you.

This balanced diet stuff is all well and good until we dig a little deeper and start listening to the health gurus out there who confuse us and make claims that don't align. You can find a talking head to tell you not to eat this-or-that macronutrient. You can find diet experts telling you certain foods will affect the body in specific ways. Even the categories themselves can be confusing. Carbohydrates are necessary for a balanced diet. However, there are both whole grains and processed sugars included in the overall macronutrient carbohydrates. To make it even more confusing, there is sugar in fruit in the form of fructose. Does this make fruit bad for you? There is a high amount of fats in nuts, and there is typically a high amount of fats in candy bars. If there are nuts in the candy bar, does that make it healthy? What if there is added protein, and it's now called a protein bar? Although some protein bars have nutritional value, the vast majority on the shelves are candy bars with protein powder added to the mix. They will advertise the number of grams of protein and some other benefits, but don't be fooled. Look at the facts on the wrapper. Most of those bars are loaded with either sugar or saturated fats (the unhealthy kind).

Use common sense and keep your food choices and beliefs simple. You know a banana is better for you than a candy bar. Eat a banana when you're hungry on-the-go. They come naturally wrapped in a biodegradable wrapper—Bonus. Do your best to stick to your macronutrient breakdown throughout your day. Eat veggies every day. Eat in moderation and try to only eat when you're actually hungry, not just bored or anxious. Some areas where moderation can be difficult are sugar, salt, cheese, alcohol, and restaurants. Pay attention not to go overboard on sugar, salt, cheese, or alcohol. When in restaurants, keep in mind their job is to serve you tasty food; they do not pay any attention to your caloric intake. That is on you. Many dieters boast that they always get a salad when eating at a restaurant. Fun fact: salads at restaurants are not healthy most of the time. The dressings are loaded with sugar, salt, and cheese. (see above items to avoid overeating) They also put way more dressing on their salads than a typical person needs.

You don't need to stop going to restaurants. And you definitely don't need to stop eating pizza loaded with an overabundance of cheese, salt, and other taste-improving substances. The change to make is instead of eating five slices of pizza, stick with two. Order your salad with the dressing on the side and only add as much as you need to make the lettuce and veggies taste better. You could also use lemon juice, olive oil, vinegar, and a little salt and pepper to replace the creamy dressings. You may not need the dressing at all as the veggies taste great. If you're at a restaurant, and you know you usually wolf down whatever is placed on the table in front of you no matter how full you get, ask for a box right away and take half the food off your plate before you get started. Now you have food for two meals instead of just one, and you've saved money too.

Fad Diets

If you're thinking about trying a new fad, check the real science behind it. A lot of the diets out there today are based on pseudo-science. This means someone is marketing a systematic way of eating to reach your goals that could logically make sense based on real science, but it has never been tested to see if someone on that diet actually gets the desired results. A few case studies may have tried the system and seen results, so they write a book, but a few anecdotal pieces of evidence do not a scientific study make. The diet that works for one person could be entirely counterproductive for another, and the truth is no one really knows what is right for all people. Our bodies are all different, and the way we respond to different meal plans can vary widely between us.

Yes, competitive bodybuilders or models trying to become more defined for a show might, on purpose, cut out all carbohydrates for a few weeks before the show or photoshoot to reduce water retention, define the muscles, and dehydrate themselves. As soon as they start eating carbs and drinking an appropriate amount of water, the definition returns to normal, and the weight comes right back as it was mostly water they lost. Most of us aren't competitive bodybuilders or models, so we don't need to cut macronutrients in the short term, and definitely don't cut any of the macronutrients out for long periods of time.

Habit-Based Solutions

To manage your calorie flow, you need to know your own weaknesses while designing processes and habits to curb them, just as discussed in the Mindset Pillar of Progress.

My weakness for food intake flares up at the end of the day. Dinner was a couple of hours ago, the kids are all in bed, we are winding down for the evening, and I am headed for the pantry. Typically, I'm not grabbing healthy food at this late in the evening because I'm craving salt or sugar. All too often, I'm standing in my pantry, thinking, "I don't really need a snack," while mindlessly reaching for tortilla chips or far worse. The fix to my problem is the easiest thing: all I have to do is brush my teeth after

I get the kids down, but before I head downstairs. I don't even think about food once my teeth are clean and breath minty fresh. Problem solved.

The key to establishing good habits is thinking ahead, and often it only requires a few minutes of thought before you start your day. If you know you're going to go out for a burger or a few beers later, don't eat as much for breakfast or lunch. You may also want to work out to burn a few extra calories and make room. If your ongoing weaknesses are eating lunch out every day, overeating during meals, or unconscious snacking, plan some time to make your lunch the night before so you can grab-and-go in the morning. Use smaller plates while eating at home as larger plates lead to greater calorie consumption[12]. Try putting your tasty snack, like potato chips, into a bowl or a separate bag before you start eating, so you don't lose track of how many handfuls you mindlessly reach for. There are habit-based solutions to almost all the issues people have with their diets. We just have to strategize upfront to integrate the healthy habits into our day and drive out the unhealthy ones.

Easy to follow food guidelines:

Add More	*Keep Low*
Protein	Saturated Fat
Fiber	Sugar

Here's how you look for the four facts to pay attention to:

Saturated fats are the unhealthy fats out there. Sugar is added to almost all processed foods as a fla-

From FDA.gov

---
12 (Smith, J. M., & Ditschun, T. L. (2009). Controlling satiety: how environmental factors influence food intake. *Trends in Food Science & Technology, 20*(6-7), 271-277.)

voring and preservative to make them last longer. Protein is found in meats, beans, nuts, legumes, and a whole host of other places. Fiber is found in fruit, vegetables, beans, and nuts. Protein and fiber are typically lacking in the American diet.

Simple Calorie Flow Metric			
If you want an easy metric to follow that will help you stick to most of the advice and information in this chapter, I recommend limiting your saturated fats and sugar intake while increasing your protein and fiber. If you can work on those two things, it will be difficult to overeat as you will feel more full and energized throughout the day.			
Saturated Fats	**Sugar**	**Protein**	**Fiber**
Saturated fats are the unhealthy fats out there.	Sugar is added to almost all processed foods as a flavoring and preservative to make them last longer. Check the labels.	Protein is the building block for muscle in the body.	Helps to regulate blood glucose levels by decreasing the rate at which we absorb sugars
Processed Meat - Salami Fatty Meats - Ribs Whole Milk Cheese Butter Chocolate Oils Most Desserts	Soda Fruit Juice Granola BBQ Sauce Many Protein Bars Canned Fruit Smoothies Cereal	Lean Meats - Chicken Beans Nuts Eggs Greek Yogurt Peanut Butter Tofu Edamame	Fruits Vegetables Beans Nuts Artichokes Broccoli Avocado Oats & Whole Grains

Cash and calorie flow are the building blocks of your financial and fitness future. If you can monitor, prioritize, and control both your eating and your spending, you will direct your health and wealth. Having extra cash at the end of the month and losing or adding weight as needed to reach your goals can send you in the right direction for your future. The next step toward your fit future is understanding how to utilize the financial and physical tools available to actualize a healthy and wealthy life: net worth and the body.

Net Worth & The Body

Now that we have the cash and calorie flow building blocks in place, let's look at the vehicles to get us to our destination. In health, we have the human body with all its moving parts. The body has muscles, bones, and joints, all working together to improve or deteriorate your health, depending on how you use it. In wealth, we have investments, loans, and other financial vehicles with all their moving parts. Your financial instruments all work together to efficiently grow or reduce your wealth, depending on how you use them. In this section, you will learn a basis of knowledge to efficiently utilize your body and net worth to produce the fitness you desire in both health and wealth

Net Worth & Investments

Your net worth is your assets (cash and investments you own) and liabilities (money you owe). It is your financial standing reference point at any given time. You determine your net worth using a balance sheet, a financial statement where we add the total value of your assets together and subtract your debts or liabilities. The resulting number is your net worth. Like weight in fitness, it doesn't give us the whole picture, but it is a place to start. At a minimum, we shoot for your net worth to be a positive number, meaning you have more assets than debts. Unlike weight for most people, your net worth is typically better when it's larger. Once you get to positive net worth, you can use different types of assets to generate a healthy, well-rounded asset base in your net worth. As they pertain to your cash flow, debts were covered in the last section. This chapter will focus on the assets and how they help you grow your net worth in your pursuit of a fit financial life.

Every type of financial investment has been designed to meet a specific need, and they all have their pros and cons. This means there is no right account or financial product out there for everyone; there is no product absolutely wrong for everyone. If you run across anyone telling you that all _____ (fill in your financial product of choice) is terrible, run away because they are trying to sell you something else. Likewise, if you come across someone telling you that you need to put all your money into _____ (fill in your financial product of choice), also run away as fast as you can.

Financial products are like tools. If you use them for the correct situation, they can get the job done effectively and efficiently. If you use the wrong tool for the job, it can be as frustrating as trying to hammer a nail with a screwdriver. Just as you could be hurt using the wrong tool for the job, you could be financially hurt using the wrong financial instrument for your goals. Each area of your asset base serves a purpose in financial planning and building your net worth.

Cash

First up is your cash. The term cash does not necessarily refer to physical dollar bills, although those count if you have them in your home or buried in your back yard. Cash refers to any asset—such as bank accounts like checking, savings, money markets, or high-yield savings accounts—guaranteed not to lose account value and able to access funds immediately without any type of penalty. At most, you may have to wait a day or two to gain access to your funds, but they will be there when you need them.

Cash is great to keep on hand for emergencies and day-to-day living expenses, but you don't want to keep too much cash in these accounts. Based on how they work, you are almost guaranteed to lose the buying power; inflation will eat away at your accounts' value over time. As the cost of goods keeps rising, your cash is worth less and less. You will want to have enough in your cash accounts to protect against emergencies, save for major expenses you know are coming up in the next two years, and fund your lifestyle. Beyond that, we will want to utilize other, more risky assets focused on growth rather than security.

Long-Term Low-Risk Investments

Although long-term, low-risk investment assets have a small chance of losing account value, you will get a bit of a return beyond that of a cash account because you give up access to the funds for a period of time. For instance, you can receive a higher rate of return in a government bond than a cash account even though the bond is backed by the full faith and credit of the U.S. Government and its ability to tax its constituents. (let's assume the US government is low-risk for the foreseeable future) Other products in this category are fixed annuities and long-term CDs. These investment vehicles are great for the ultra-conservative investor or someone who knows how much money they will need by a given time and wants to ensure they have it. For instance, if you need $10,000 in three years, and there is a three-year CD offered for 4%, you would need to put roughly $8,890 into the CD today to ensure you have the $10,000 when you need it. These investments will mostly keep up with inflation under normal circumstances, but they won't outperform inflation over a decade or more. Again, with lower risk comes lower expected returns, and these investments have minimal risk.

Secondary Market Investments

As you take on a bit more risk in your balance sheet, you will start investing in secondary markets. A secondary market is any market where you can buy and sell an investment to other investors for a price you both agree upon. Think of the real estate market, as that's the secondary market most people are familiar with. You can buy a house, live in it or not, keep it for as long as you like, and sell it to another person later. The goal is to buy your home for a lower price than you sell it later, right?

The same is true in the bond or the stock market. You can buy a bond or a stock, keep it for as long as you like, and sell it to another person later. The goal as an investor in these markets is the same: you want to sell your investments for more than you paid for them. The differences between the types of investment markets are the levels and causes of volatility in these secondary markets. It is believed by most that the real estate market is reasonably safe. With real estate, you own tangible property, which makes some less nervous about their investment. While the buying and selling of stocks and bonds work similarly to real estate, stocks and bonds are not real property. You can't hold them in your hand, so they aren't as intuitive for newcomers.

Real Estate
Many investors like the idea of real estate as an investment vehicle because they can see, touch, and experience their investment. People more easily understand real estate as they understand what it means to own a home in which to live. While real estate can be an excellent investment, the comparison to a traditional diversified portfolio is not apples to apples.

Real estate performs much like other real assets, such as gold, over time. Typically, inflation, or the increase in the price of goods sold in the marketplace, is a good benchmark for real estate growth. Although your house is an enormous good, it is still sold in the marketplace. You can expect somewhere between a 2-4% growth rate over time. When faced with such low growth rates, the first thing people will say is, "I bought my house eight years ago for $250,000, and now it's worth $480,000." You are correct that your home could grow at an annualized 8.5% rate over eight years.

However, 2010 through 2018 was a booming time for real estate and is definitely not a full market cycle. My Dad has owned the home I grew up in since the end of 1983. He bought the house for $99,000, and it is worth $345,000 35 years later. His home value growth rate over a few market cycles is 3.6%, close to the inflation rate over that same period. By comparison, if my dad had invested $99,000 on January 1, 1984, in the S&P 500 index, he would have just over $1,700,000, based on price increase alone over that same time, without including reinvesting dividends from the underlying stocks.

The reason investing in real estate can be a great investment is the leveraging of dollars through a mortgage. Here's the example from above to illustrate the idea:

If we use mortgage debt to purchase a home in an increasing value market, we are using a relatively small amount of money out of the buyer's pocket to obtain a highly valued asset. The following is an example of what the home above would be worth putting 20% down in cash and financed the rest:

Home Purchase Price…………..$250,000
Down Payment……………..….$50,000
Mortgage Amount………….....…$200,000
Mortgage Interest Rate……….…..….5% (amortized)
Sale Price……………………….$480,000
Holding Period……………..…..8 years
Remaining Mortgage at Sale……$171,706
Equity in Home………………….$308,294

Some further assumptions for added costs:

Taxes and Insurance……………$32,000 (4,000 per year)
Repairs and Maintenance………..$16,000 (2,000 per year)
Rental income……………………….$0
Total Interest Paid……………..$74,775

After taking into account the $50,000 down payment, $28,294 of principal payments, $74,775 in interest paid, taxes and insurance at $32,000, and repairs and maintenance of $16,000 over the eight years, you've invested a total cash amount of $201,069.

The total return on your investment:
Home value – Total Invested – Remaining Mortgage = Return on Investment
    $480,000 – $201,069 – $171,706 = $107,225 or 7.52% annualized

This is a beautiful story of how real estate can work out well for someone. However, there is a significant risk of account value loss that comes with this investment style, as seen in the recession of 2008. When assets are purchased with a loan, there is a risk that the asset's value could drop below the amount of the loan itself. Combine this value loss with the need to move or a loss of income, and you're not going to sell for more than you purchased the home. You could still owe money on the house you no longer own.

The better apples-to-apples comparison between real estate with loans and the stock market is buying stocks and bonds on margin. If you're buying on margin, you are actually borrowing someone else's money to invest in a financial vehicle you think will increase in value more than the interest you're being charged. Once the investment has increased, you take the proceeds and pay off the loan. You just made a lot more money than you would have if investing all your own funds, but you took on a lot more risk to do it.

The risk shows up if the underlying investment you've purchased goes down in value. Now you've lost someone else's money because you took a loan, used the funds, and can't pay back the loan with the sale of your investment. You had better find the money elsewhere, or you'll be in hot water. You could lose your home or other assets to make up the difference.

Bonds

The vocabulary around the bond market makes understanding how bonds work a bit confusing. Finance people talk about 'buying' a bond from the company 'offering' the bond. You're not really buying anything, and they aren't offering anything. Technically, you are giving a loan to the company asking for money. In return for your loan, the company will give you interest, known as a coupon. If you hold the bond from the initial offering to the full term of the loan, the company offering the bond will give you your initial investment back and all the interest payments along the way. Where bonds get a bit tricky is buying and selling *between* the initial offering and the loan's full term. When a company asks for money, they will give you a coupon rate—the rate of interest paid to you—in line with the level of risk you're taking as an investor (another example of more risk, more opportunity for reward). That means a "highly rated company"—a company with a high credit score which is likely to repay their loan and not default—will give you a coupon rate higher than the bank savings accounts or long-term CD's, but not much higher. A company offering a bond with a higher risk of not getting paid back (also known as a junk or high-yield bond) will give you a higher coupon rate than the investment-grade company because you're taking more risk as an investor. Without getting into too much financial mumbo jumbo, the cost to buy a bond on the secondary market from another investor is dependent on the rates you could get in your low-risk investments at the bank. You have to take more risk to own a bond than you do in a bank account. If you could get a higher rate in your savings account today than the bond is paying, the value of that bond to you as a buyer has gone down significantly. The extra interest you would earn has gone down while the risk you have to take is still the same as the company issuing the bond has the same risk of possibly not paying you back.

The value of a bond can be confusing, so here's an example:

- You purchase a 5% coupon bond for $1,000 when your cash investments are paying 2%.

The bond is paying you an extra 3% above cash for the added risk that your loan could go unpaid if the company fails.

- A year later, cash rates have risen to 3%. Your bond is now only earning 2% above the cash rates as the coupon rate has stayed level at 5%.
- If you were to sell your bond to a different investor at this time, they would pay you less than the $1,000 you paid as their return for the same risk is only 2% as opposed to the 3% difference when you purchased the bond.

For this reason, and a few others we won't get into right now, buying and selling bonds inside the offering and the full-term dates can be volatile when market interest rates are changing. Hopefully, the diagram below utilizing the example above will help:

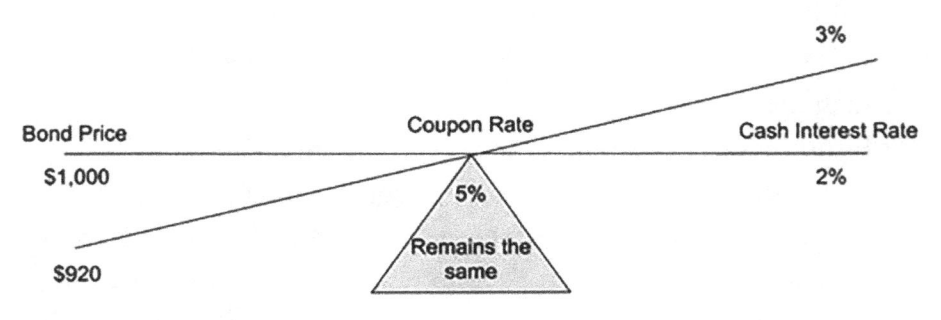

Bond Price	Coupon Rate	Cash Interest Rate
$1,000	5%	2%
$920	Remains the same	3%

Stock Market

The stock market is a bit more straightforward as you are actually buying something. When you buy a stock, you are literally buying ownership in a company. If you own one share of ABC Company, and they have 100 shares in the hands of investors representing 40% ownership of their company, you own .4% of ABC Company. Of course, one share of a company on the major stock exchange is a much smaller percentage of ownership than that, but you get the idea.

When you own part of a company, you participate in what happens to that company. If they make money and become a bigger, stronger company, you make money, and the price of your stock goes up; therefore, the value of your investment goes up. On the other hand, if the company you own makes big mistakes and goes into bankruptcy, you could lose the full value of your initial investment. This risk is what scares some investors from investing in the stock market. Still, it is also the reason the overall stock market generally outperforms inflation over long periods.

Common Question: What do news channels mean by "the market"?

When the American media discuss the market, they are typically talking about one of two indices that have little to do with the overall health of the market or economy. They are either talking about the Dow Jones Industrial Average ("the Dow") or the S&P 500.

The Dow is an index consisting of 30 large companies across a swath of American industries. There are two significant issues with using the Dow to represent the entire market. The first is only 30 companies are represented in the index. In contrast, there are thousands of companies one can invest in, so only assessing 30 of them will never be a full representation of the market. The second main issue is the fact the Dow index is price-weighted. That price weighting uses the price of one share for each of the 30 companies included in the index and adds them all up to equal the index's value. Consequently, companies with higher-priced stocks have a larger weighting in the index. If the largest company's share changes by 1% in a day and the smallest company's share changes by 1%, they will have different impacts on the index's overall return for that day.

The **S&P 500** Index ranks and weighs the top 500 companies in the New York Stock Exchange (NYSE) and the Nasdaq Stock Market (NASDAQ) by size, or market capitalization. While representing 500 companies is better than 30, it is still not an accurate representation of the overall market. The main problem with the S&P 500, though, is the fact it is also weighted. Because of this weighting, 20% of the companies held in the index make up 80% of its performance.

These two indices are the basis of all the media coverage out there for the U.S. stock market. When the talking heads scream the sky is falling, the overall stock market may not be that bad. This disconnect between media messages and the market's real value can create a misconception of what is happening in the global marketplace. The media could be reporting the market is taking off based on the value of these indices. If an average American is watching the news and owns a portfolio that is allocated and diversified in international stocks, international bonds, domestic bonds, and other holdings that are not at all represented by "the market." The U.S. indices the news anchors talk about could be up while their own portfolio is down, and that can be frustrating. Remember, the "market" is just an index that gives us one measurement of how the U.S. stock market is performing; as with most individual measurements, both indices are flawed and only a fraction of the full picture.

Don't pay attention to *anything* the journalists say regarding market performance. The financial news anchors mostly have degrees in journalism, not economics. In most cases, when they are emotional and reactive to something in the market, they're just reading off a card to sell some ads. Please keep that in mind.

A Risk-Appropriate Balanced Portfolio

Now that you know how the secondary market works, we can get into the next level of your balance sheet. When you have a non-retirement goal, but it is several years away, maybe even decades away, how do you save for it? A balanced portfolio of stocks, bonds, and other investments matching your time horizon and risk tolerance for your savings goal is recommended. If you want to build a deck on the back of your home in a few years, you will want to be more conservative with those funds. The market could take a turn for the worse at any given time in that period. On the other hand, if you want a vacation home in Hawaii before you retire but still fifteen to twenty years from now, you can be pretty aggressive with your investments until the purchase time approaches.

The way you gauge the risk in a portfolio is the mix between stocks and bonds, or equity- and fixed-income-style investments. If you're in 30% or less of equity investments like stocks and 70% or more in the fixed-income style, that's a lower risk portfolio built for the 3- to 5-year goals. Between a 30-70% and 70-30% stock to bond distribution constitutes a mid-range of risk for your 5- to 15-year goals. 70% or more equity with 30% or less in fixed income would be a higher risk for your long-term, 15-plus-year goals.

Non-retirement-type goals like saving for a new home, building additions to your home, or saving for your kids' college future are some goals you might pursue using a risk-appropriate portfolio. You could also save for future health expenses or set aside funds to have ready for financial goals that don't exist just yet. You could use several different account types for savings, depending on the purpose. These accounts are known as non-qualified accounts, as they are not set aside for retirement. Some examples include individual or joint accounts for the most liquidity, trust accounts to dictate exactly what the funds are for, or 529 college savings plans for education-based goals. Of course, there are pros and cons to every account type, so there's not a right answer for every single goal. This is one reason financial planners are vital as they can guide you in evaluating which investment vehicle and level of risk are appropriate for your unique goals.

Retirement Accounts

You can use retirement accounts, also known as qualified accounts, for your long-term goals after age 59.5. Certain tax benefits are associated with designated retirement accounts, so utilizing them for your long-term objectives can be advantageous if used correctly. Retirement accounts are titled one of two ways: a Traditional or Roth retirement account. For this book's purposes, we won't go into detail on the alphanumeric soup that is 401(k), 403(b), IRA, SEP, SIMPLE, etc., but they are either a Roth or a Traditional retirement account. You'll want to know how each works so you can plan ahead.

Within these retirement accounts, you can receive tax deductions, tax-deferred growth, or tax-free withdrawals. A **tax deduction** is a benefit that reduces your annual income, and you'll find an example of this tax deduction below. **Tax-deferred growth** allows your invested retirement assets to grow every year without having to pay the annual tax haircut you would in a typical individual or joint account. When one of the normal individual or joint account investment grows and is sold or rebalanced, you have to pay taxes on that growth as it is 'realized' to you in the form of capital gains or dividends every year. In a tax-deferred account, your assets are not taxed until you make withdraws. Therefore those assets compound on themselves over long periods, so you can accumulate more retirement assets than you would in a non-retirement account over the same time.

Finally, **tax-free withdrawals** are exactly what they sound like; you don't have to pay taxes when you pull the funds out of your account. The following table shows which retirement account gets which benefit.

Type of Account	Tax Deduction	Tax Deferral	Tax-Free Withdrawals
Traditional	Yes	Yes	No Ordinary Income
Roth	No Earned Income	Yes	Yes
Individual or Joint Account (Non-Qualified)	No Earned Income	No Capital Gains on growth Dividend tax on dividend	No Capital Gains on growth

The benefits offered in both Traditional and Roth retirement accounts are mathematically the same *if* you are in the same tax bracket when you make your money as when you withdraw your money. The problem is the chances of that happening are slim-to-none. You'll make more or less money in retirement, or the tax brackets will change between now and then. You have some control over your income amounts, but you have no control over tax brackets (unless you're in Congress, and if you are, please advocate for real-world fitness and financial education to be required in the public-school curriculum).

Have both Traditional and Roth accounts available to you when you get to retirement. You can pull from your Traditional taxable funds when you're in a low-income tax year, and you can pull from your Roth non-taxable funds when you're in a high-income tax year. This way, you have some level of control over your tax situation in the future while taking advantage of some tax breaks today.

Alternative Investments

Once you have built up the basics within your financial plan, you may find yourself looking to even more risky investments. These are typically not as transparent, not well-diversified, or not at all liquid. These assets include real estate you own but do not live in (rental properties), businesses you own but don't work in, investment vehicles like real estate investment trusts (REITs) that buy and manage commercial or multi-family properties, business development companies (BDCs) that give loans to private companies, or managed limited partnerships (MLPs) that tax investors like a partnership while allowing investment in companies similar to a financial security. These assets are considered "alternatives" because they provide an investor with an alternative to the traditional secondary markets. Alternatives are typically risky, so I do not recommend them until other goals are funded. Once we have grown your diversified, balanced portfolio to a level that will pay for your base lifestyle in retirement, you can use assets like these to diversify further and add risk—where risk can be taken—to the portfolio.

Common Misconception: Gold is safe

It's not. Facts:

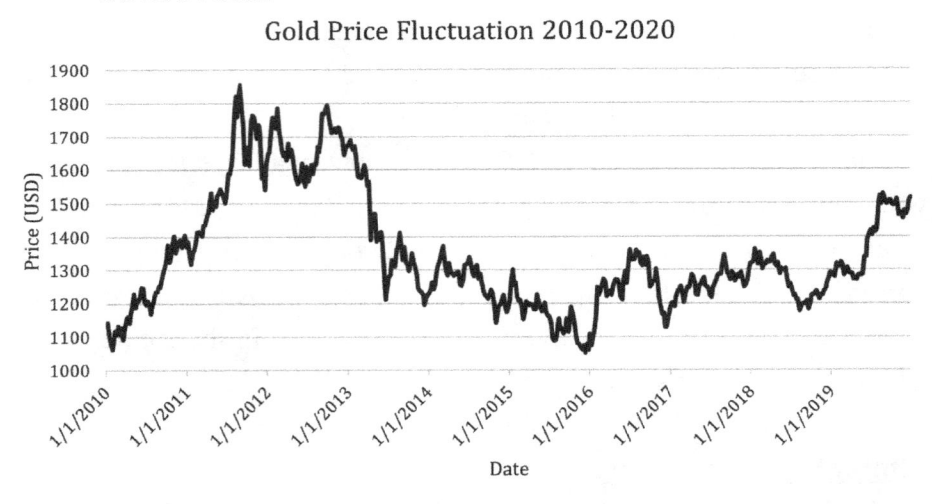

Gold Price Fluctuation 2010-2020

[Line chart showing gold price in USD from 1/1/2010 to 1/1/2019, ranging from about 1000 to 1900, with a peak near 1800-1900 in mid-2011, declining to lows near 1050 around late 2015, and recovering toward 1500 by 2019.]

This is the ten-year chart for the performance of gold ending on December 31, 2019. If you were to purchase gold in August 2011 when many investors were flocking to gold, you would have taken a ride down nearly 50% by the end of 2016 and be down just over 20% about eight years later. There is always a risk if you have the opportunity for a return in investing.

Your net worth is a number to know and pay attention to as you keep growing in your financial life. It is the best way to measure where you stand at any given time. As your net worth grows, you will have more assets set aside for different goals in different accounts and investment vehicles; keep track of where these assets are and what kind of risk you're taking for the possible rewards. Consider what your funds are for, when you will need them, and that your investment risk can increase as your time horizon increases. Use investment vehicles appropriate for your goals and the saving time frame to meet those goals.

Asset Type	**Strategy**	**Investment**
Emergency Savings	3-6 months of non-discretionary expenses in cash vehicles	Checking, Savings, Money Market
Long-term, Low-Risk	Utilize safer, somewhat illiquid investments for goals less than 3 years away.	CDs, Treasury/government securities
Risk-Appropriate Balanced Portfolio	The longer the time horizon, the more risk you can take.	Nonretirement accounts - Asset allocation portfolio of stocks, bonds, mutual funds, or exchange-traded funds.
Retirement Accounts	Similar to the strategy above, but with tax advantages. Access before 59.5 years old is limited.	Traditional or Roth accounts with an asset allocation matching the risk of your time horizon to retirement needs.

The Body

Your body consists of a whole mess of complex stuff (very scientific). Our mix of bones, organs, muscle, fat, and water helps us stay upright and complete our day-to-day activities. Every part of the systems that make up the human body work together, so we can do everything from playing complex sports to video games on the couch.

A considerable amount of body mass is made up of bones and organs. A lot is going on in there, and our various body parts all serve a purpose. The body's components detailed for the fitness purpose of this book are fat and muscle. Fitness explores how fat and muscle affect a person in their everyday health throughout their lifetime. Taking care of the body is enjoyable once the effects of getting stronger, fitting better into clothing, and having more energy throughout the day start to show up. Although an active focus on your health will push your comfort zone as you get started, the ends will justify the means.

Before we get to the workouts and how to improve your fitness, let's start with some of the basic body knowledge. As we covered before, fat is physically stored energy in the body. Muscles can utilize that stored energy to create movement.

Muscles

Your muscles are built to move your bones through a range of motion while providing stored energy so your body can move when the brain asks it to. The two major types of muscle in our bodies are fast-twitch muscles and endurance muscles. The **fast-twitch muscles** help accomplish such tasks as heavy lifting or jumping. They can quickly create a lot of power, but they also get tired relatively fast and require quite a bit of recovery. Your pectorals, latissimus dorsi, biceps, triceps, quadriceps, calves, and other well-known muscles are all fast-twitch muscles. You can train your fast-twitch muscles to complete endurance tasks, like an ultra-marathoner and other long-distance athletes do, but these muscles are still fast-twitch in type. While they've been trained not to fatigue as fast, they will get tired eventually.

On the other hand, your **endurance muscles** will help you do a task for a long time without fatigue. The most well-known endurance muscle is your heart. It beats all day and all night without getting tired. Your diaphragm also helps you expand and contract your lungs all day and night without getting tired. You can work these muscles by increasing your heart rate and your oxygen intake during a workout, but even if you don't train the endurance muscles, they will go on working for a long time.

The more muscle you have in your body, the more energy your body needs to support itself. Every extra pound of muscle in an average-sized person's body needs an extra 50 calories per day while at rest to sustain itself. This means, if you grow your muscles, you can burn more calories even while sitting on the couch.

Common Question: Why do I gain weight when I start a workout plan?

There's an adage that muscle weighs more than fat. It's true, but not the whole story. Muscle is far denser than fat. Five pounds of muscle will take up less room than five pounds of fat. The problem with the adage 'muscle weighs more than fat' is the inference that muscle and fat are mutually exclusive.

You cannot turn fat into muscle. The person who figures that out will be as sought after as the alchemist who turns lead into gold. You can burn fat and lose it. You can build muscle. You can both lose fat and build muscle simultaneously if you are diligent and focused on your diet while pushing yourself on resistance training. But more often than not, most of us are either losing fat or gaining muscle at any given time with exercise.

When you first begin a workout regimen, you will be building muscle. Even while running or doing cardio only, you need your leg muscles, hip muscles, foot and ankle muscles, and even your core muscles to be trained and ready. When you start with your first run, your muscles know to evolve to prepare you for the next run. Your body will be thinking, "It seems like we're going to keep running from time to time. We had better prepare the muscles so we can run farther and more often." Then the body builds up the muscles to support the activity the next time around.

Most people see an increase in their muscle mass before any noticeable differences in fat reduction. As a result, weight scale numbers go up. If you let it, a heavier weight measurement can be frustrating and defeating. Don't let it. It is just your body acclimating itself to your new routine. Let the body do what it needs to do. The results you want will come quickly and balance out once the habits are established and the body adjusts.

A muscle group is multiple muscles within a body region working together around a joint to support your motion. Think of a bicep curl. The muscle groups are your arms and shoulders. Starting with a dumbbell hand weight at your hip height with arms outstretched, your bicep muscle contracts to pull the weight up toward your shoulder. Your triceps muscle elongates to allow the arm to hold the weight and build up the energy that will allow you to return to the start position, like a rubber band stretching out and contracting back to its original place. The biceps and triceps have different jobs, but they are both needed to complete the movement. While the arm comes back to the outstretched starting position with the weights by your hips, the biceps stretch back out, and the triceps contract as the weight comes down. Once again, the two muscles work together to lower the hand weight in a controlled fashion. There are also specific muscles in the group necessary for stabilization, balance, and support. During the curl, the shoulder has to be strong and stable to keep the arms from swinging back and forth. You've got to work all the different muscles within a group for true functional strength and fitness.

Although your muscles are built to hold you upright with good posture, it's easy to develop tight or loose muscles due to repetitive stress or continually holding them in an unnatural state. Many who sit at a desk all day for work already experience this by having tight hip flexors, hamstrings, and IT bands, typically causing pain in the lower back. If you feel joint or muscle soreness, many times the pain comes from one side of a complementary muscle group being over tightened while the other is loose. For instance, since my car accident, my spine has been a bit out of alignment. If I sit with poor posture for too long, my chest muscles will strain and contract to pull my bones back into the proper alignment and "fix" my posture. As far as I can tell (as an average Joe attached to all these muscles and bones), my upper back muscles ache, just like when a headache puts me out of commission for an hour or so. The sensations can also come about if I overtrain one muscle in the group without training the other muscles to keep the group balanced and the tightness at bay.

Your posture can cause issues with your muscles, but you can also use your posture to determine the areas of improvement needed in your fitness. If your hip flexors are rigid from sitting all day, you may have what is known as an anterior pelvic tilt. That's just a fancy way of saying the top of your pelvis tilts toward the front of your body, which means your lumbar spine, or lower back, will arch to keep your center of gravity beneath you, typically causing back pain. Try stretching your hip flexors regularly and training your core and glutes to help your pelvis tilt back to equilibrium.

Your muscles, when properly trained, fed, and rested, will grow. Muscle growth takes some additional body chemistry, but training, protein, and sleep are the main ingredients. If you want to grow your muscles, do the same as you do with a portfolio looking for growth; you have to take a risk. You have to push the muscle to some level of exhaustion for it to recover and grow. Calling the growth of muscle "building muscle" is a great descriptor, but you have to realize muscle is built by repairing muscle that has been broken. You push that muscle to the limits, and it breaks down a bit. Then you feed it, let it rest, and recover. The next time you push the muscle, it will be more prepared for the test.

The Workout

Because there are so many different ways to work out, many people avoid the gym altogether because of paralysis by analysis. All those machines, classes, and people who "know what they're doing while I don't know anything" can be daunting. The truth is most of those people have no clue what they're doing either. Someone once showed them how to use a particular machine, or a coach showed them a lifting routine years ago, and they're still doing the same routine. So, it's okay; you have nothing to fear. Just get in there.

Hopefully, some basic understanding of the different types of workouts will help. Just like financial products, no workouts or pieces of equipment in the gym are inherently flawed. Some techniques, equipment, and programs are better than others for certain types of people, but they all have their merits.

Cardio

Cardio can help with fat loss, but aerobic exercise develops and improves your heart and whole-body cardiovascular system. The current recommendation from the World Health Organization is to do 150 minutes of activity a week. That's 30 minutes a day, five days a week, to support a healthy heart. Those 150 minutes could be filled with walking, running, time on the elliptical machine, cleaning the house, playing with your kids or dog actively, or even engaged in adult sports. It doesn't have to be a slog you *do every week*. You can make your cardio fun and fit into your life. Grab a coworker, preferably one you like, and go for a walk during your coffee break rather than standing around the water cooler.

Even if all you're trying to do is gain big muscles, you still need to train your heart to avoid burying those muscles in an early coffin.

Weight and Resistance Training
Weight and resistance training are other types of workouts everyone needs. You can lift heavy weights, furniture, cement blocks, anything heavy to bulk up, or you can lift lighter weights with more repetitions to grow your strength. Either way, challenge your muscles regularly. Resistance training is good for weight-loss, building muscle, and increasing energy. It's vital for your bone density as a challenged bone will lose density much slower as we age than an unchallenged one.

If you're a beginner, consider hiring a trainer to show you the proper form while lifting weights. Using improper form is the most common cause of injury in the gym. If your gym has a trainer on–hand, consulting on the floor, they would be happy to show you around as long as you're willing to listen to the spiel for purchasing some training sessions. A few sessions to get you started on the right path is a good idea if you can afford it. There are times in your fitness life when some professional direction and advice can kick-start your results, and beginning a new resistance program is one of those times.

<u>Body Weight Training</u>
Another type of resistance training is bodyweight training. Exercise doesn't get more functional than bodyweight training. Regardless of your phase in life, chances are you have to carry your body around wherever you go. Some push-ups, pull-ups, squats, and lunges are exercises you can do nearly anywhere with minimal equipment, and the benefits are immense. If you need help to use your body weight for a full-body workout, TRX training can be a fun change of pace. TRX was created by a Navy Seal and consists of a strap system and exercises to go along with them to challenge your body in different ways. You can also make

certain exercises easier and available, regardless of your level of fitness right now. As you grow stronger, you can modify the exercises to increase the intensity and challenge yourself.

Yoga and Pilates

Two common forms of exercise you can use to build strength, flexibility, and balance are yoga and Pilates. I love yoga because it enhances core strength, promotes mindfulness, and supports recovery during a resistance-training regimen. As we age, yoga is even more beneficial because one of the biggest threats to our health as we get older is the possibility of a fall or not being able to react fast enough to a changing environment. While accidents can happen at any time, remaining strong, balanced, and flexible can also prevent situations from arising.

Pilates is another workout routine like yoga, but it is more rigorous and strength-focused. Pilates is all about engaging every part of your core, from your hips and hip flexors to your middle back. Many trainers will attest that Pilates is an effective fitness regime for core strength and mobility.

High-Intensity Interval Training

HIIT, or High-Intensity Interval Training, allows you to get an effective workout quickly. The idea is to do a cardio-style workout to raise your heart rate above 70% of your maximum for a relatively short period, or interval. Then you take a brief break to let your heart rate come back down before you jump into the kick-your-butt mode again. The intervals will vary based on the program and instructor, but there are programs with one-minute high intensity and fifteen seconds rest and some with 10 minutes on and a minute rest. The workout intensity can land anywhere on the difficulty spectrum, depending on your ability. You have to be in great shape to stay in a high heart rate zone for ten minutes. This type of regimen—like CrossFit and Insanity—is gaining popularity in the US as people have less and less time to devote to their fitness.

The downside of these workouts is they are not for beginners; you must be in great cardiovascular shape to keep up with the pace. You also have to be careful to maintain proper form on your exercises to ensure you don't hurt yourself as you get more and more fatigued. If you participate in a high-intensity interval training program, please check your ego at the door, as you probably won't be able to lift as much as you can at the gym, where weightlifting happens in sets with frequent breaks in-between. When your heart is pumping, you're starving your muscles of oxygen, so the fatigue sets in much faster. Don't let your pride talk you into hurting yourself by pushing yourself too hard.

Recovery

Just as important as the workouts themselves is the recovery. For your muscles to grow stronger, you have to let them rest. This goes for biceps and your other "beach" muscles, as well as the necessary muscles that pump your heart and help you keep your balance. You have to sleep, drink water, feed your body good food, and let your muscles rest. Resting your muscles means not pushing muscle groups that have been worked recently and are still sore. That recovery could be a day on the couch binging Netflix to take it easy or working your legs today to let your upper body rest. Now we will focus on your sleep.

The hormones that help your body recover are released during deep sleep, so you have to sleep long enough to get through full cycles. Shoot for 7-9 continuous hours of sleep every night. Everyone is a little different here, too. I can sleep seven and a half hours a night and feel great. Others can sleep 6 hours a night and feel great, and some can sleep 10 hours a night and not feel rested. Know yourself and get what you need to be at your best.

Sleep Ritual List
If you're one of those people who struggle with sleep, there are a few things you can do to create a more restful environment.

Sleep Environment	**Pre-Sleep Ritual**
Cool to cold – 65-66 degrees is ideal	Epsom salt bath
Dark as possible	No blue light from phones, TV, or computers for one hour before sleep
Sound machine if necessary	Herbal tea – just not so much you have to use the bathroom in the middle of the night
No technology near the bed – use an old-fashioned alarm clock	Stretching and breathing exercises can calm the mind and the body

Have you ever had the experience of being half-awake in the middle of the night, and when you check the time on your phone, you notice a new email notification? Now you're interested…oh, and now you're awake. Great, it's two o'clock in the morning, and you're thinking about work. Pick up a cheap, old-school alarm clock to wake you in the morning. If your cheap alarm clock keeps the middle-of-the-night phone scenario from happening even one time, it's worth it.

To train yourself and begin a new routine, you could plug your phone in away from your bed and take an Epsom salt bath to stay away from it. You'll have to be disciplined the first few nights to not look at your phone or turn on your TV after your bath, but you'll get in a rhythm after a while. As an added bonus, this routine can also reduce stress.

> **Common Misconception: I will make up for my lack of sleep on the weekend**
>
> It's a myth that you can make up for not sleeping during the week by sleeping in on the weekends. You cannot make up for lost sleep because the effects of a poor night's sleep are immediate. The next day you will experience the negative impacts on your memory, attention, eyesight, and motor abilities. You need those motor abilities and mental functions to perform your job and your exercise routine, so hurry off to bed early enough to sleep through the night.

All bodies are different and require different amounts of work and rest, as well as respond to different types of exercise. This broad health information is meant to be used as a starting place, but you will likely need to do some trial and error with workout routines, rest and recovery, and other aspects of your fitness to find what works for you. There is no one *right* way, so find what your body needs to stay healthy. Devise a fun, safe fitness routine you can stick with for an extended period of time. These routines are lifestyle choices, not some hard boot camp to survive in order to get quick (and temporary) results. The lasting results will come from a sustained effort and appreciation for your health in your daily decisions. Which leads us to: how do we measure our progress?

Measuring Progress

While working toward a goal seemingly far in the future, it can be easy to lose your way from time to time. If you lose the plot too much at any given time, you could really set back your progress. I've found it is helpful to measure my progress through the months and years to keep me motivated and on track to my future goals. In fitness, there are times you will look in the mirror and ask, "why am I doing all this when it's not even working?" We call these plateaus—where it feels as if your progress has flattened out, and you're working hard only to stay at the same place. If you can look back at measurements and pictures, you'll see your plan is working, and you've already come a long way. In wealth, you can utilize one of the online platforms to track your net worth to take a look at your history, or you can keep track of the numbers yourself on a spreadsheet, but looking back a few years to see how far you've come is helpful when feeling stuck. Plateaus happen mentally in finance. When you notice yourself asking, "How will I ever get to my retirement goal?" then referring to your measurements will remind and encourage you. This chapter will go over different data points you can measure in both health and wealth to keep you motivated while moving ahead.

Measurements of Wealth

In wealth, you'll want to track two primary data points and work to keep them both positive: net worth and net cash flow. You can also use the fundamental planning ratios to start; the emergency fund, consumer debt payment, housing debt, all debt, and retirement savings ratios are guidelines set forth by the Certified Financial Planner Board (CFPB). The CFPB ratios are a place to start measuring your financial status as they measure your current financial reality in the key categories of cash savings, retirement savings, and debt management. If you have too much debt, the ratios will tell you so. If you don't have enough emergency funds, you can determine how much more you need to save. If you're not saving enough for your future retirement income, your savings ratio will average out too low. In the beginning stages of planning, these ratios will steer you to a good start:

Emergency Fund Ratio

This ratio tells you how many months of savings you have on hand in case of an emergency. The recommendation is 3-6 months of your non-discretionary expenses on hand at any given time.

Cash on Hand
Monthly Non-Discretionary Expenses

Consumer Debt Payment Ratio

The goal of this ratio is to keep you from overcommitting your current income for past consumption. The CFPB recommends staying below 20% consumer debt-to-income to ensure you're not paying for your life now with too much of tomorrow's income.

All Monthly Loan Payments Outside of a Mortgage
Net Income per Month

Housing Debt Ratio

This ratio is built to assure you are not house-rich and cash-poor. The ideal recommended range to not have more house than your budget can allow is below 28%.

Mortgage Payment
(Principal, Interest, Taxes, and Insurance or PITI)
Gross Income per Month

All Debt Ratio

The all debt ratio is exactly what it sounds like. What percentage of your gross income is going to pay for debt of all kinds? The ideal range to live within your means and not use too much debt to finance your life, including housing, student, and consumer debt, is less than 36%.

Gross Income per Month
All Debt Payments per Month

Retirement Savings Ratio

Are you saving enough? Each person will be different in their savings needs based on how much they already have and what lifestyle they want in retirement. Try to save 10% of your income for retirement, but that recommendation is only for those with thirty years or more until retirement or well on their way with a lot already saved. If you're getting a later start or feel behind in your retirement savings, the ratio needs to be more like 15 to 20% or more.

$$\frac{\textit{Total Monthly Retirement Contributions}}{\textit{Gross Income per Month}}$$

Once you have all your ratios at the recommended levels, you'll want to begin funding your goals appropriately. If you don't know how to use a financial calculator, you can easily access calculators all over the web to determine your savings need for any goal. There are resources for calculators like this on www.fitfinancialapproach.com. If you'd like to add a deck to your home that will cost $15,000 in 3 years, you can change the terms of the calculator to return your needed savings amount. If you'd like to save toward a trip around the world in 10 years, estimate the cost of such a trip and adjust the time on the calculator to determine your annual savings to reach that goal. First, we need to calculate your future cost of living. The following are the steps with an example. If you're not great at algebra, you may want to find a free financial calculator on my website to work this out without all the math below.

Calculating Your Future Cost of Living

You can use the following future value equation to determine the cost of the future lifestyle you just quantified in today's dollars:

$FV = PV*(1 + i)^n$

FV is future value, *PV* is present value, *i* is interest, and *n* is the number of years.

You will need values for your future lifestyle in today's dollars (PV), inflation (*i*), and the number of years until retirement (*n*).

- ❏ *PV* - use an estimate of your preferred lifestyle in retirement in today's dollars
  - ○ *Example: We want to have a $6,000 per month lifestyle in retirement.*
  - ○ *$6,000 x 12 equals a $72,000 annual cost.*

- ❏ *i* - use values for inflation somewhere between 2.5% and 4.5%. 3.5% is a reasonable, conservative estimate for our example where you have a long time until retirement. If your time horizon is fewer years, use a percentage closer to the current inflation rate.
  - ○ *Example: With a long time until retirement, we will use 3.5%.*

- ❏ *n* – use the number of years you have until you're actually going to retire, regardless of your full retirement age for social security.
  - ○ *Example: We have 30 years until retirement in this case.*

Let's calculate your future retirement income need:

$FV = PV*(1 + i)^n$

$FV = 72,000 * (1 + .035)^{30}$

$FV = 72,000 * (1.035)^{30}$

$FV = 72{,}000 * (2.8068)$

$FV = \$202{,}089.15$

$202,089.15 per year will buy the same lifestyle in 30 years that $72,000 per year pays for today.

If you can find a financial calculator (one with N, I/Y, PV, PMT, and FV buttons), you can use that to calculate your future need as well. You have to enter four of the five variables on those calculators before you can compute the final one.

Let's use our example:

- ❏ N = 30 years
- ❏ I/Y = 3.5 percent
- ❏ PV = 72,000 dollars
- ❏ PMT = 0 (we're not adding to the value but just forecasting the current cost of living)
- ❏ FV =?

When you calculate FV, you will get the same $202,089.15 as above. Now that we have the total annual amount your preferred future could cost you, we have to know how much you will need to start saving annually to create that income in the future.

Calculating Your Future Retirement "Nest Egg" Need

If you divide your total annual future cost by the percentage of your nest egg you will withdraw annually, it will give you the total amount you need to have saved for retirement. In this rudimentary way of determining your future savings goal, we are not considering social security or taxes, so you can use the 5% withdrawal rate just to be in the ballpark. You can be more conservative by choosing 4 or 3%, but that's not necessary for this example. Most people will have social security or something similar to offset their asset need in retirement. (And, no... social security is not going away as the news would have you think – see common misconception at the end of this chapter.)

- ❏ *Example:* If, Annual Future Cost / Withdraw Rate = Total Savings Need
- ❏ Then, $202,089.15 divided by 5% equals $4,041,783.

$4,041,783 is the nest egg you will need to live your lifestyle in the future. This number is in its future value, so remember that $4 million 30 years from now is not the same as $4 million today. Again, this also does not consider Social Security or any other pensions you may have, so you can either offset your future income need before going through this process or use the horseshoes and hand grenades method where *almost* is a good enough measurement. The latter works just fine in most cases. Now we have to determine how much you need to save every year to get there.

Calculating Your Monthly Savings Need

Once again, we will use the formula and the financial calculator. We will use the following equation:

$$FV_{Ann} = CF\left[\frac{(1+i)^n - 1}{i}\right]$$

- ❏ FV_{Ann} is the future value of an annuity. This is the term given to annual payments added to find the future value. We will use the nest egg value from above.
  - ○ *Example: We will use $4,041,783*

- i is interest this time. Instead of using inflation, we will use a rate at which we expect our investments to grow. Stay in the 6-8% range to remain conservative over time. A good rule to follow is if you have ten years, use 6%. If you have twenty years, use 7%. If you have thirty or more years, use 8%.
  - Example: Because we have 30 years in this example, we can comfortably use 8% as our growth rate.

- n is the same number of years used above to determine the lifestyle amount with inflation.
  - Example: 30 years

- CF is representative of cash flows, and we will be solving for this variable to find how much your annual, and then monthly, savings needs to be to reach your nest egg value.

Let's solve the equation:

$$FV_{Ann} = CF \left[\frac{(1+i)^n - 1}{i} \right]$$

$$4{,}041{,}783 = CF \left[\frac{1.08^{30} - 1}{.08} \right]$$

$$4{,}041{,}783 = CF \left[\frac{9.0627}{.08} \right]$$

$$4{,}041{,}783 = CF[113.2832]$$

$$\frac{4{,}041{,}783}{113.2832} = CF$$

$$35{,}678.57 = CF$$

Okay, Let's go back to our financial calculator and try it again:

- N = 30
- I/Y = 8
- PV = 0
- PMT =?
- FV = 4,041,783

Now when we calculate PMT, we will get -35,678.57. For the purposes of this exercise, you can ignore the negative, and you can see the number is the same as above.

We just have to make the annual investment number monthly by dividing by twelve, and we get 35,678.57/12 = $2,973.21. Our example planner would have to start saving $2,973.21 per month right away to be able to retire how they would like in 30 years, given a 3.5% rate of inflation and an 8% growth rate in his investments. Most people will be nowhere near the financial ability to save this amount today, and they likely will be able to save way more than that number later. That's okay. Remember, this number is just a guideline to let you know where you are in your journey today.

- *Example:* Our example shows you will need to save $2,973.21 every month for the next 30 years while getting an 8% rate of return on your investments to accumulate over $4M. If you start with $650 per month now and keep your savings rate the same for the next 30 years at 8% growth, you will already be at nearly $1 million in this scenario. The goal for this number is to know you need to start saving as much as you can and continue to increase your savings rate over time as your income increases.

This exercise isn't mean to scare you, although sometimes we need a good scare to make positive changes. This information empowers you to make better saving and spending decisions moving forward. Go through this process of determining your savings rate once a year to see how you're doing with your savings increases. If you can keep increasing the amount you set aside for your goals, your net worth will add up over time. Continue tracking your financial ratios quarterly or semi-annually to ensure you are getting and staying on track with the accepted standards. If you have these numbers to reflect on when you feel discouraged or tired of saving, the progress you have made will keep you motivated.

> **Common Misconception: Social Security isn't going to be there for me**
>
> First of all, older Americans rely on Social Security. Secondly, they vote. It would be political suicide for elected officials in the legislative or executive branches to allow Social Security to fail.
>
> Let's say no one fixed Social Security, and there were no changes moving forward. Eventually, the trust paying the Social Security benefit would run out of money; that's correct. That does not mean that the U.S. Government stops collecting Social Security taxes. The government would take the tax money they bring in and immediately pay whatever percentage they can to those collecting an income. Retirees might not get the full benefit they were promised, but they would still receive a percentage of their expected income for decades before this system became unsustainable.
>
> The worst-case scenario is the income recipients receive less than they anticipated, but the Social Security pension is not going away unless it is entirely replaced with something else. Too many Americans rely on Social Security pension as their primary source of retirement funds to let it disappear.

Measurements of Health

You will experience plateaus during your journey to a healthy lifestyle, so be mentally prepared. The best way to tackle a plateau is with the verifiable knowledge your body and health are progressing even if the visual results you want aren't yet showing in the mirror. The success measures can help you see what the mirror does not reflect; be ready for these plateaus by consistently tracking your progress.

Body Mass Index (BMI)

Despite the fact Body Mass Index, or BMI, is the best we have for measuring both health and obesity, it's an awful method because it is over-simplified. BMI is merely a measure of weight versus height to determine if you weigh too much for how tall you are. BMI worked better in the '70s and before when people rarely lifted weights or trained their bodies. These days, with fitness being a part of most Americans' lives to some extent, BMI has become a less valuable measure of health. The more muscle mass someone adds to their body through proper fitness training, the more they will weigh for their height. As we've gone over earlier in the book, weight measurements only tell you how much force you apply to the ground. Your weight doesn't tell you whether that weight consists of fat, muscle, bones, water, or anything else. If you have a low amount of fat and high muscle, you could be healthy and still have an obese BMI level. A doctor once told me I was obese based on BMI after weighing me while wearing a full suit and tie. She didn't even have me take my shoes off. Between my resistance training and my heavy clothes, of course, I am categorized as obese based on BMI ratings, but I didn't have an abundance of fat on my body to cause health issues.

Don't put too much stock in a BMI rating as you will improve your fitness, and the measure will be meaningless. If you care to know what your BMI is, there are many online calculators you can use. You can go to www.fitfinancialapproach.com for some resources. For your reference, a healthy BMI is between 18.5-25, and anything over 30 is considered obese. Again, don't be upset with the results if your weight consists of muscle…or clothes. Body fat percentage is a far better measure of a healthy person.

Body Fat Percentage
A much better measurement for someone with a higher level of fitness is measuring body fat percentage. The problem with this measurement is the propensity for error. Typically, personal trainers are not accurate with the skin fold pinchers (sometimes off by 5% or more). The bioelectrical impedance devices can vary based on how hydrated you are or other environmental or physical variables at the time of the test. If you can afford a displacement tank, MRI machine, or CT scanner, then body fat percentage is a far better measure. I am one of those who get frustrated with inaccurate information, but I'm also too frugal to spend thousands to get an accurate body fat measurement. The low-cost device for electrical impedance body fat measurement used once a week can track the trend and be sufficient. A healthy body fat percentage for men is between 14-20%. For women, a healthy range is between 17-24%

Waist Size Measurement
A quick-and-easy measure for health is the waist size measurement. Use a soft measuring tape to measure your waist between your hipbone and ribs. Don't push your core muscles out, and don't suck them in. Just relax. If you're a male and your measurement is over 40 inches or a non-pregnant female with over 35 inches, then you most likely have excess fat around your organs that could lead to health issues (some of which are heart disease, high blood pressure, diabetes, sleep apnea, and certain types of cancer.) Of course, these numbers are just guidelines, and you could be a naturally larger-framed individual who has a broader

waist but low body fat. Or you could be a petite person with a smaller waist and plenty of fat to spare. Again, generalizations this simple can't be right all the time.

Bench Press One Rep Maximum

To measure your strength, you can use the bench press one-rep maximum. If you're working to achieve weight-lifting goals and increase lean body mass, the bench press one-rep maximum helps track your increased muscle size, which is directly tied to how much weight you can lift. (Lifting heavy weights in fewer repetitions will build larger muscles.) If, however, you're performing resistance training to maintain bone mass, fight muscle loss as you age, or build a healthy level of strength, you probably never need to know this reference point.

There are challenges to this measurement method, not the least of which is how do you do a one-rep max safely? You will need a spotter to attempt the one-rep max. Be warmed-up but not fatigued when you try a one-rep maximum lift, as you can easily injure yourself with this exercise. This strength measurement isn't necessary for most, but powerlifters swear by it. It could be dangerous as you risk pulling a muscle, hurting a joint, or dropping the weight on yourself. Unless you're under the watch of a professional and focused on building overall strength and power, don't perform the one-rep max lift. Still, if you really want to know where you are with the measurement, there are some great tables with a reference for one rep maximum bench press weights at different body weights with age discounting online. You can also find estimators where you can input several different resistance exercises with the weight you use and reps you can complete to estimate your one-rep max. Again, you can go to www.fitfinancialapproach.com for a list of resources. In any case, *only* attempt a one-repetition maximum lift with a qualified spotter in a safe environment.

Body measurements

Make it a point to measure your arms, legs, waist, hips, neck, and chest once a month to track progress as your fitness increases. Body measurements allow you to see improvements even when the scale may be telling you otherwise. For instance, if you're gaining muscle, your weight may be up, which can be disheartening. With body measurements, you can see when your arms and chest have increased in size while your waist and hips decreased. People don't see the number on your scale; they see the inches have come off. Again, losing fat is far more important than losing weight, so worry more about the inches than the pounds.

Flexibility

As we get older, a vital measure is our flexibility. As you age, you can lose flexibility if you don't continue to work on it. Flexibility can be measured at home with the sit-and-reach. You can use a step in your house and a ruler. Place your feet against the step with your legs on the floor and knees extended. This is your starting point. Place the ruler on top of the step, hanging over the ledge. The ruler will be parallel to your legs and hang above or between your feet. Now you will bend at the waist and reach as far as you can three times, recording the distance you can reach beyond your toes each time. If you cannot reach past your toes, record the distance to your toes from where your fingers touched the ruler and make the number negative. Average the three measurements for your score.

If you're a male adult, 2.5 inches or better is good flexibility, and anything less than -3 inches is considered poor flexibility. For an adult female, above 4.5 inches is good, and below -2.5 inches is poor flexibility. Like the others, this test is not infallible. How often do you really need to stretch your fingers to your toes in a real-world situation? Because the sit-and-reach has been used around the world for decades, there is a ton of data to compare ourselves against. Chances are, if you're flexible in reaching to your toes, you'll be flexible in other, more functional areas as well, like twisting your head to check a blind spot before merging into traffic.

Blood Pressure

Blood pressure can be another good tracking test. You can take your BP levels at the grocery store, doctor's office, or with a personal device. The target for your upper number, or *systolic level*, is below 120, and your lower number, *diastolic*, is below 80. Currently, the medical community deems any numbers over 130-over-80 to be considered high blood pressure. Untreated high blood pressure can put a lot of stress on your cardiovascular system and lead to heart attack, stroke, erectile dysfunction, and many other issues.

Blood Sugar

You can use your blood sugar levels to determine your health as well. These tests require a blood draw at a lab or doctor's office. The goal is to be under 100 mg/dL (milligrams per deciliter) before eating and under 140 mg/dL a couple of hours after eating. If you have diabetes, these numbers will differ, so see your doctor to set your targets and ensure you're in a healthy range for you.

Lipid Profile

Finally, your lipid profile, or cholesterol and triglyceride levels, are indicators of your overall health, especially the risk of a heart attack. Total cholesterol is comprised of both your low-density lipoprotein (LDL-the bad type) and high-density lipoprotein (HDL-the good type) levels. Combined, you're shooting for these levels to be less than 200mg/dL, with HDL being higher than 60mg/dL. Triglycerides at a healthy level will be lower than 150 mg/dL. Higher levels could lead to arterial blockages, heart attack, or stroke. This test is completed using a blood draw, so please see your doctor for guidance.

If all you do is take one of these measures and link your overall health to that measurement, you could be completely ignoring other health concerns, some of which may creep up without your knowledge. Track at least a few of these measures as you age. When I was younger, I didn't even track my weight; all I had to do was feel good to know I was doing the right things. As I've gotten older, many times, while seemingly on track, given my weight and body fat percentage, my blood pressure was high due to stress, lack of sleep, and dehydration. Unchecked, blood pressure could lead to deteriorating health. Although you may not need to check your lipid levels or blood sugar levels annually, whenever you get a doctor's wellness check, ask for the bloodwork results to ensure those measures are in line with the recommended levels.

Measuring your progress carries you through your plateaus. It can also be helpful when measuring progress toward a goal you've set. Reflect on where you started and celebrate the progress you've made toward your goals. Seeing the percentage increase will keep you focused. Know yourself and what metric keeps you dedicated to a goal, so you can measure that metric to stay on track in both health and wealth. If you need help determining what to measure, refer to the lists below.

Wealth		
Measurement	**Measuring**	**Ideal**
Net Worth	Total assets v. debts	Positive
Emergency Fund	Liquidity, Safety	3-6 months non-discretionary expenses
Consumer Debt	Debt percentage other than housing	Below 20%
Housing Debt	Percentage of income dedicated to housing	Below 28%
All Debt	Debt-to-income ratio	Below 36%
Retirement Savings Rate	Percentage of income saved for retirement	10% minimum, 15-20% ideal

Health		
Measurement	**Measuring**	**Ideal**
Bodyfat %	Overall body makeup	M – 14-20% F – 17-24%
Waist Size	Excess body fat	M – 40 inches or less F – 35 inches or less
Bench Press 1 Rep Max	Power	? – for increased muscle size, more is better
Body Measurements	Body size	Depends on the body and your goals
Sit-and-Reach	Flexibility	M – 2.5 inches+ F – 4.5 inches+
Blood Pressure	Circulatory System	120/80 is ideal
Blood Sugar	Diabetes	Under 100 mg/dL before eating 140 mg/dL a couple hours after eating
Cholesterol	Heart health	HDL above 60 mg/dL LDL below 150 mg/dL The combined total below 200 mg/dL

Even when tracking and measuring our progress, life sometimes doesn't go according to plan. Outside factors can derail your progress, and unexpected events can take us backward, away from our goals. What can we do to prepare for the unanticipated?

Protection for Your Plan

When setting a plan, most people only think about what it will take to reach the goal in their current situation. But life changes, sometimes abruptly and without notice. If you don't protect your plan, you could be thrown completely off track. What do you do when you're on your way to reaching your goal of 16% body fat, and you break your leg slipping on ice in the grocery store parking lot? Now you can't walk, let alone complete sustained cardio workouts. What do you do five years out from buying your vacation home when your company files for bankruptcy and has to lay you off? Or what if you have a disability that affects both your health and wealth at the same time? Weigh your risks and embed protection for your plan so you can survive the abrupt issues that could crop up along your journey.

Financial Protection

When developing a financial plan, you have to protect your plan from the events that could derail your financial future. A plan can be derailed by an unexpected loss of a job, a health issue, or an untimely death. The hard part of protection is knowing what to protect from and how much protection to have. Typically, financial protection comes in one of three forms:

1. You have enough money to cover any issues that could arise.
2. You have insurance to protect against the scenarios you cannot afford.
3. You do nothing to protect yourself and hope for the best.

Don't do number three, if you can avoid it.

Although protection is essential, there is a risk of over-protecting yourself. You don't want to end up with a fully protected life and no life to protect because a considerable percentage of your assets are being applied to premium payments. As an example, when you first start in your earning life and form the habits of saving and protecting, there typically isn't much to protect yet. At 24, I didn't have a wife or kids. I didn't own my home. I was totally invincible, and I was never going to get sick. What did I need with a death benefit? Not much, really.

You'll want to find a balance to protect against the most significant risks for the life phase you're in. And, because your needs will change throughout your life, review your protection plan at least annually. The following sections will cover different types of protection you can use to safeguard your plan from unforeseen circumstances.

Health Insurance

No matter what period of life you are in, **health insurance** is a must. At all times, you want to be covered in case of an unexpected medical event, even if you can only afford insurance with really high deductibles. It is better to owe *some* money to a hospital when you're injured or sick than owe *everything*.

When you're younger, typically 20s to mid-30s, and rarely visit the doctor, look into an HSA, or Health Savings Account. HSAs are available with a high deductible health plan and allow you to save money for future health expenses with a tax deduction when the funds are contributed, tax-deferred growth as the funds grow in value, and tax-free withdrawals when you use the funds for qualified health expenses. HSAs are the only vehicles that allow you to get all three tax benefits in one account, so use them for growth when you're young. When you need to use your medical benefits at certain times in life, the HSA is less advantageous as the funds do not have time to grow before they need to be used.

As you get older and need more medical care, you may want a lower deductible plan such as an HMO or PPO—provided by an employer or purchased individually—that covers more health services because you'll actually use the coverage. With three kids, our family uses our insurance all the time. When my kids were little, and something looked/smelled/sounded/felt funny, they went to the doctor. Sometimes our kids used the medical care benefits because they got hurt trying to keep up with their siblings and fell against the stone steps forehead first. These things happen. Because we use our benefits often, we selected a lower deductible, more expensive, and a more robust health care package through my employer. If you're self-employed, typically, your health insurance plan will cost more than a group plan. Still, individual plans are available and completely necessary if you're not covered some other way.

Life Insurance

There are two main types of life insurance: term and permanent. Term insurance covers you for a certain term of time (hence the name) and is cheap. Term coverage is appropriate when someone has a good reason to have extra protection for a period in their life. For instance, when a client has a baby, I recommend adding a 20 to 25-year term policy to cover the child's expenses and college if you're not around to earn and save their whole life. Permanent insurance—also known as whole, universal, or variable life—can last your entire life rather than merely a term of time. Besides the death benefit, there are many reasons to utilize permanent life insurance in a financial plan. Some reasons could be living benefits to protect against possible illness or injury or access to tax-advantaged cash value later in life.

At 24-years-old, although I didn't need death benefit, I started a permanent life insurance policy with living benefit riders that would pay me in the event I had a terminal or chronic illness. (Some insurance companies even offer life insurance policies with critical illness benefits that pay for cancer, heart attacks, and strokes) Many talking heads will advise you to buy term and invest the rest, but the math comparison between investing the rest in investments and utilizing cash value for retirement isn't obviously in favor of the buy term invest the rest strategy. You won't have as much money accumulated inside a life insurance policy as you would have in a Roth IRA, but your Roth IRA isn't going to pay for your chronic illness or untimely death either. By starting young with a permanent life policy, you can have life-long protection, grow some equity, and eventually receive a tax-free income stream that will give you options in retirement if the tool is properly used. While young and healthy, the cost of permanent insurance will generally be low. As you get older, the cost goes up, and you won't qualify any easier the longer you wait, so start the life insurance policy as soon as you can afford it as it accomplishes three goals with one product.

As you start adulting and move into mid-career, you may decide to marry, have children, or buy a house. As you add more and more responsibility to your plate, now the death benefit is needed. You probably need even more coverage than the policy you purchased when young and didn't need death benefit, so it may be time to add a cheap term policy to protect your family from an unforeseen loss of income. We all know people pass away sometimes. You don't expect it, but yes, it could happen to you. Please protect your family.

I have seen a thirty-something father left with four young kids trying to figure out how to keep life relatively (as much as is possible in a situation like this) the same after their mother died unexpectedly from brain cancer. He always thought his income was high enough to take care of everything, so he didn't get coverage on his wife. The problem is he wasn't ready to go back to work for a few months after the woman he loved was taken from him too early. He needed to grieve, but he didn't have the chance because his family needed the money. He also had to find a child-care solution and someone to help out around the house, and he had to learn how to take care of all the responsibilities his wife had managed that he wasn't even aware of. Life after her passing was awful, and it burdened him, his kids, his parents, his in-laws, and many of his friends. They were happy to help, but he didn't like being an inconvenience.

On the other hand, I've watched a friend pass from aggressive cancer in his early 40's. He left behind his wife and three young kids, but he was fully protected. With the insurance proceeds, she paid off their house so the kids could maintain some relative level of consistency. She could also afford to stay home from work for as long as she needed to grieve and figure out what the new normal would look like for their current situation. Although most of us would prefer neither of these situations, I'd choose the second scenario if I had to choose one. No one gets to choose who or when tragedy hits, but I guarantee someone you know will have something like this happen to them. When term policies are so cheap, would you be willing to take the chance that a catastrophe happens to you first? I sure wouldn't.

Disability Insurance

In your mid-career, you may start making more money, and as with most people, start taking on more responsibility. More responsibility leads to the need for consistent income. Disability coverage will pay you if you are ever unable to complete the tasks required for your job. If you don't have a fully-funded emergency fund, look into disability coverage. If your income increases and you have not had a chance to bump up the emergency fund, you need disability income coverage.

The consideration with disability coverage is knowing whether your policy covers your own occupation or any occupation. If you choose a policy that covers any occupation, so long as you can perform work anywhere, you will not get paid. In most cases, you will want the own occupation coverage—even though a disability policy with own occupation coverage is more expensive than any occupation coverage—because as it will pay you when you lose your income due to a disability and unable to perform the function of your current occupation. Once you fully fund your emergency fund, which may be quite a bit of assets between cash and conservative investments, you can drop or reduce the disability coverage.

Umbrella Policies

Other adult decisions like buying a house, expensive cars, and wedding rings lead to required protections as well. You will need to investigate good homeowners, car, personal property, and umbrella coverage.

The first three are straight-forward. If you own stuff you can't afford to replace easily, protect it with insurance. If you own a home where people could get hurt on your property or a car that could hit things (they all can...believe me, I've tested it a few times), you'll need to have adequate coverage for the situations that could arise. If you are in a car accident that happens to be your fault and you cause a medical issue—which sometimes happens when you have a few tons of metal objects smacking into one another at high rates of speed—your $25,000 or $50,000 in car insurance coverage for liability will not be enough. If the injured party sues you for the amount over the insurance, you could be on the hook. This is why I always recommend clients purchase an umbrella policy.

Umbrella policies cover expenses that occur above your standard coverage for property and casualty insurance. Your umbrella coverage would kick in benefits if the medical bills piled up beyond your car insurance coverage amounts. If you get sued for different reasons, your umbrella coverage could cover your legal fees and other costs. To obtain umbrella coverage, your other P&C policies must be up to certain minimum limits set by the insurance company, which is also good for your protection plan. You do not want to be under-insured for your property and casualty. The state minimums for P&C are typically not enough coverage, but the umbrella minimums are generally a better gauge of how much is sufficient. You will want to start with at least $1 million in umbrella coverage. The more prominent insurance companies can typically insure you for up to $5 million, which would sufficiently cover most people, but some companies can go higher if you need more than that.

Property and Casualty Insurance

To find property and casualty coverage, shop around. Just going to the proprietary, or captive insurance, agent down the street in your local strip mall could cost you, as they only sell their own company's plans. Get a quote there, but then take that quote to an independent agent who can shop around multiple insurance companies and get you a better deal. Shop your deal each year as well. Property and casualty policies have similar benefits across the spectrum of competing companies. If you search around, you can often find a better price for the same coverage. If you have your own company, multiple properties, or any outside-the-box needs, take your business to an independent agent who specializes in your type of situation and can find gaps in coverage for your financial plan.

Long Term Care

There are many examples where millions of dollars disappear in a staggeringly short time due to a long-term care need, which is why protection always includes advanced medical cost planning. The average cost of long-term care is thousands per month. A memory-care medical issue like dementia or Alzheimer's can cost the most while also lasting longer because the mind deteriorates faster than the body.

There are several ways to prepare for long-term care needs, but none of them are perfect. If you have enough money to self-insure—which can take millions—then keep the money in an investment geared for long-term needs, taking on slightly more risk in the market. You may not need to access all of the funds for quite a while after full retirement, so those funds need to keep up with inflation.

If like most people, you cannot self-insure, there are several options. Stand-alone long-term care insurance is not always the best choice as those policies can be expensive, and in most cases, if you don't use the policy, you will have paid a lot of money in premiums for no reason. That being said, if you are particularly worried about the need for care, you will want to weigh the costs against the benefits to ensure you are getting what you want. Some policies cover in-home care; some don't.

Some have a cost-of-living adjustment built into the benefit; some don't. Another option to consider is the waiting period—the number of days after needing care before the benefit of your policy will start paying you. Typically, the waiting periods can range from 30-90 days, and the difference in the waiting period can have a significant effect on the cost of insurance. If you start planning young enough, advanced medical cost protection could be a life insurance policy with certain living benefits attached. You can get terminal, chronic, and critical illness riders attached to specific policies. They will pay you from your death benefit to cover for specified illnesses, effectively using your death benefit while you're still alive. The downfall is you would not have a death benefit for your heirs as you would use the benefit while alive; you'll have to weigh that decision for yourself. Using life insurance with living benefits when appropriate in a financial plan can be a fantastic benefit, as they can cover the need for death-benefit *or* advanced medical costs with one policy. Any time one dollar is working on two or more different plan elements, that's a win. Long-term care protection is not always fun to talk about with your financial planner or anyone else for that matter, but planning ahead for the eventuality of your declining health could make or break your wealth. Push through the challenging conversation and set the right protection plan for you and your family within your overall financial plan.

Legal Structures

Protection doesn't just mean insurance for the tragic life events that could blow up a financial plan. You also need to think of the legal documents that can be used to support a plan. See an attorney to help with this aspect of the plan if you haven't already.

You need a fully executed **power of attorney for health** and a **power of attorney for financial** decision-making, just in case. If anything happens to you, you don't want your family to have to wait for the court to approve or appoint someone to make financial or medical decisions for you. If you're married, don't think your spouse will automatically be that person, either. How often are you and your spouse in a car where an accident could incapacitate you both? Plan for the contingencies of life and take the time to think through who you want to make decisions on your behalf if you were not able.

Another document you want your attorney to draft for you is a **living will or medical directive**. This document addresses the different decisions your family could face in the event of an accident or illness. How long do you want to be fed through a tube? How long do you want to be plugged into machines? How many times do you want to be resuscitated if your heart stops? The living will removes the burden of these decisions. You don't want your wife or kids to battle with whether to tell the doctor to "Pull the plug." How awful. Don't put your family in that position. Pay the money to have someone draft your living will appropriately, so your wishes are clear, and your family doesn't have to go through mental torture.

Laws are different from state to state. Go to an attorney who is knowledgeable in the estate and family arena for your state of residence. If you reside in multiple states, tell your attorney so they can plan accordingly.

Protection is a difficult part of any financial plan. You can get all the coverages and protect your plan to the highest levels, and a memory care issue could still wipe out your entire nest egg. You could also never buy any insurance and, one day, fall off a cliff with your last thought being, "I'm really glad I didn't listen to that long-term care insurance salesman." The point is, you never know what's going to happen. You have to find the right amount of coverage for each of these areas for yourself. You don't want to over-protect or under-protect. You can have too much coverage and pay so much in premiums you can't enjoy your cash flow. You can also pay too little in premiums and not adequately protect your plan. Just think through your specific situation and the likelihood of different events, and then you can determine where your assets and concentration need to be. If all of your extended family passed away in their 50's, you might want to buy life insurance just in case you fall in line with the family lineage. If a couple of your grandparents required long-term care for more than a few years, you could have a likelihood of needing care. Your lifestyle could play a role, as well. If your grandparents all died of heart disease because they never worked out a day in their life and ate nothing but butter and drank beer, you may be okay if you take care of yourself. While none of these assessments will tell you exactly which coverages to have, you can find a happy medium where you feel comfortable protecting your assets and family from most, but not all, possible events in life. There are many highly qualified people out there who would be happy to help with this analysis and conversation.

Health Protection

Mobility *is* health protection. The better your mobility, the better protected you are from incidents like falls, joint sprains, muscle pulls, or soreness. When you're young, you can recover from any of these quickly; you may not even realize you hurt something. As we age, recovery can take much longer, and the pain impacts more areas of your life when you're older. Being able to catch yourself with a quick movement to grab a railing or the ability to reach just a bit farther without hurting yourself can mean the difference between a close-call and a hospital stay.

As we age, the body starts to fall apart; your memory will start to go, metabolism slows down a bit, testosterone levels and lean muscle mass will fall, calcium levels lower, and a whole host of other fun things occur. You have some control, however, of the rates at which the body falls apart. If you're already on top of your fitness and keeping up with your healthy eating habits, you won't see a decline in your faculties as quickly as others might. You've seen those people who look as if they are not a day over 45, but they're actually almost 60. Those are the people who kept their healthy habits and continued to focus on their fitness. It has been shown physical fitness also helps to maintain mental wellness. Resistance training helps keep bone density high against the loss of calcium. Testosterone levels and metabolism can decrease much slower if you continue to challenge them into your older ages. As we get older, our mobility can deteriorate. The three keys to maintaining mobility – flexibility, balance, and core strength –protect our health as these three components help us move where and how we want safely.

Flexibility

Maintaining flexibility throughout your life allows you to continue to move with a full range of motion and protects your joints. When a muscle is tight for extended periods, it will pull on the insertion point where the muscle is attached to the bone. For many muscles, these insertion points are near joints. The constant pressure of your muscle continually pulling on the bone in a particular direction can add stress to the joint itself and pull the joint out of alignment. Over time, major issues can arise and require several surgeries or even a joint replacement to "fix" or alleviate the problem. Always warm-up before stretching. Walk or move around a bit before you start stretching, so you're not lengthening cold muscles. Think of trying to stretch a frozen rubber band where it breaks rather than stretches. Once you're fully in your stretching session, stop and hold the stretch to work the length of the muscles, then switch sides to stretch both sides of a muscle group. If you stretch your hamstrings, also stretch your quadriceps. If you stretch your chest, also stretch your back. This practice will keep your muscles balanced over time and not overly stretched or tightened.

Balance

Balance becomes more and more important as we age to reduce the risk of being hurt in a fall. Older people often fall and break bones due to poor balance and low bone density. Your bone density will remain higher with resistance training, and you'll be far less likely to fall if you challenge your balance regularly. Using equipment like inflated exercise balls, balance pads, and off-balance exercises can train your balance and help you remain standing instead of falling over. You can also stand on one leg while brushing your teeth twice a day (switch legs halfway through) or stay standing when you put on your shoes; that'll get you working your balance every day.

Core Strength

Finally, your core strength is arguably the #1 strength you can have. Our core muscles, including the muscles in our abs, hips, glutes, lower back, and spinal support, are used in almost every movement we make. If you've ever thrown your lower back out or pulled a hip flexor, you know exactly how often those muscles are used because you can't shift in your seat without feeling the injury. Honestly, regardless of how old you are, start working on your core now. You can use planks—where you support your whole body on your elbows and toes, keeping your back and glutes as straight as possible. Crunches are good, but you also need to work your low back, obliques, and transverse abdominals through twisting exercises. Roman twists are a great exercise to work the other core muscles; you sit with your feet off the ground, leaning your shoulders back, and rotate your shoulders side to side. You can hold a dumbbell for added resistance. Bicycle twists are great, too; lie on your back with your feet six inches off the ground and your hands at your temples with elbows pointed away from your body. Bring your opposite elbow and knee together as close as possible, then go back to the starting position and repeat with the other side. If you work through those exercises alone, your core will gain strength quickly.

Make sure you are regularly working on your flexibility, balance, and core strength. Regular yoga can enhance your abilities in all these areas, especially the older you get. I love yoga, personally, but I don't yet spend a lot of time practicing yoga as I'm more into cardio and weights for the moment. As I get older, I plan to incorporate a yoga practice into my fitness routine. I'd even like to become a yogi for my retirement job, which is a great segue into the next section on planning for your future wealth and wellness.

> **Common Question: Why do my knees hurt?**
>
> Most likely, it's because you sit too much. A muscle—commonly known as the I.T. band—runs down the side of our thighs, connecting our hips to our knees. When we sit, the I.T. band tightens up. If that muscle overexerts, it will start pulling your knee out of a proper, comfortable position and cause pain.
>
> You can do a few things to counteract this problem, not the least of which is sit less. Get a standing desk; take breaks to walk around the office every so often; request standing meetings with your team. Take a thirty-minute walk for your weekly check-in with a team member. It will be one of your most productive meetings every week.
>
> A few simple stretches throughout the day will help to lengthen this muscle and alleviate the strain on your knees. One of the best is the **twisting triangle stretch**. Standing with one foot in front of your body at normal hip-width, reach the opposite hand from the foot that's in front forward and lean down to touch the floor (or a ball or chair if you're not as flexible). Take the hand on the same side of your body to the foot in front and reach toward the ceiling, twisting your body and stretching the IT band. Hold this position

for 15-20 seconds. My Achilles tendon usually feels like it is on fire when I do this stretch, but the twisting triangle stretch helps alleviate my back pain and my knee pain by stretching all the muscles on the side of my legs. I try to do this stretch at least once a day, on both sides of my body, but do this stretch as often as you feel it is beneficial.

For some, a **simple quad stretch** will do. Just stand on one leg (use a chair or wall for balance if you need) and grab the other foot behind your body. Keep your knees together and your chest up. Again, hold the stretch for 15-20 seconds on each side. You can grab the foot with your opposite hand and pull it to the side of your body as well if you have good balance. If not, stick with the chair or wall. This stretches a different part of the same muscle group. The simple quad stretch is far easier to complete multiple times a day. You can even experience the benefits while wearing your work clothes.

Another way to ease some of the pain is **self-myofascial release (foam rolling).** You'll need a foam roller and can purchase one at any store where sporting goods are sold. While on your side, lay the top of your hip on the foam roller with your forearm or hand on the ground, holding you steady. Now roll the foam roller down the side of your leg. When you feel spots that hurt, stop rolling, and let the pain settle in. Once the pain lessens, you can keep rolling and stopping until you get to another knot where you stop again. It usually takes 20-30 seconds at least to feel the pain lessen. Repeat this until you get to the top of your knee. The self-myofascial release can feel somewhat painful like a deep tissue massage, but well worth it just the same.

Of course, you'll have to do the above stretches and foam rolling for a while to mitigate the pain. It could take weeks or even months. You've probably built this tightness up over time, and it will take time to teach your body where stasis is again. If the problem persists, you may have a more intense issue, and it's probably time to see a doctor or physical therapist.

Protection requires we set aside some of our assets or training time to prepare our financial and fitness plan for possible future mishaps. We've covered different insurance protections where you pay a premium to offload the risk of an unexpected event to an insurance company. To protect your body, we've also covered basic fitness recommendations that focus on mobility rather than building muscle or losing fat. In both cases, the time and money set aside are well worth the resources if you encounter unexpected events. The hope is you never need any of these coverages, but inevitably most people will need at least one of them, and many need more, so have a well-protected plan.

Wealth		
Protection	**Covers**	**Coverage Needed**
Health Insurance	Illness and Injury	An appropriate deductible for your situation
Life Insurance	Unexpected death	Minimum 5x annual income
Disability Insurance	Short- or Long-term disability	Situational
Property and Casualty Insurance (P&C)	Car, house, jewelry, rental, boat, etc.	Enough to qualify for an umbrella policy
Umbrella Policy	Anything above P&C coverage up to the coverage amount	Minimum $1 million in coverage
Long Term Care Insurance (LTC)	Chronic illness requiring medical support	Situational
Legal Documents	Decision making while alive and after passing	4 documents – will, living will, power of attorney for health, and power of attorney for finances

Health		
Protection	**Covers**	**Coverage Needed**
Flexibility	Range of motion	Stretching daily or do yoga
Balance	Unexpected falls	Stand on one leg, sit on an exercise ball and lift your feet, or do yoga
Core Strength	Postural alignment	As strong as possible – planks, crunches, twists, etc.

Leaving a Legacy

Whether you choose to or not, you will leave a legacy. It may not be monetary, but people will remember you for something. Wouldn't you prefer to consider ahead of time what you want those you care about to remember about you? Otherwise, they get to choose, and that could go sideways. After a parent's death, many heirs feel they don't want to leave such a mess for their kids as it was such a pain to deal with the estate. Don't let your heirs think you were a pain after you're gone. While you are alive, you have control over how your beneficiaries experience managing your estate, and you have the opportunity to make your family's transition as easy as possible after your death. The following are some ways to do just that:

Leaving Your Wealth Legacy

You may want to leave your kids or other heirs some money, good memories, a house, your stuff, or any number of other things, but there are a few considerations before you slap their names on a will or beneficiary form. Similar to your income, it's not about how much you leave to your heirs, but how much they actually receive. You could bequeath a million-dollar account, but if you haven't structured your wealth to account for income taxes, the account might only be worth $800,000 or less, depending on your beneficiary's tax bracket. When you're in retirement, you are typically in a low-tax bracket. When parents pass, their kids are typically in their waning working years. So, heirs have to take withdrawals from their parents' taxable retirement accounts while typically in the highest tax brackets they've ever had. This can be a severe drag on the legacy you wanted to leave.

Account Types

The following are the basics of how various accounts work in the transition of losing a family member:

Traditional IRA

If the beneficiary is a spouse, they can take over as the IRA owner and continue as if the account was their own. If there is a non-spouse beneficiary, we have to create a beneficiary IRA that requires a distribution, so Uncle Sam can get his taxes. These withdrawals will be taxed as income added on top of their income. The laws change in this area periodically, and as of right now, these accounts must be fully liquidated within ten years of the date of death.

Roth IRA

Spousal beneficiaries have the same benefits as Traditional IRA's; they take over as if it was their own this whole time. Non-spousal beneficiaries have to create a beneficiary Roth IRA. Withdrawals are required to limit the amount of non-taxable funds accumulating over multiple generations, but they will not be taxed.

Non-retirement Accounts

The assets in a non-retirement account receive a step-up in cost basis. This is a technical term, so let's break it down. Cost basis is essentially the amount of money on which you have already paid taxes. Over time, you could accumulate gains on that money, and once you sell the original holding along with gains, you will pay taxes on the growth as either short-term or long-term capital gains. If you pass away without selling that holding, the government gives your heirs a pass on those taxes; your heirs take over the account with a cost basis equivalent to the account value on the date of your death. This can be a massive benefit for highly appreciated assets like houses or stocks.

Non-qualified Annuities
Non-qualified annuity is a fancy way of saying an annuity is held outside of retirement accounts. They receive tax deferral for account owners while in the growth phase, which can benefit during working years, but you will reap the significant benefits of the tax deferral while in the lower tax brackets in retirement. Many don't realize this, but your heirs will have to pay taxes at earned income rates if they inherit a non-qualified annuity with an account value greater than its cost basis. Again, the cost basis is the amount of money on which you've already paid taxes. Leaving one of these accounts to your heirs takes a benefit to you and uses it to screw your kids. Don't do that.

Tax-Effective Legacy Strategies
Since we're on the same page (literally and figuratively), let's talk about a few strategies that could be beneficial for leaving an effective legacy. It's a bit morbid to think about your own death, but it's the only guaranteed event in life. So, it's something we need to plan for.

Let's start with this basic situation: You've worked your whole life, birthed a few kids, raised your children, saved your money, retired, and now you're getting up there in years. Your kids are probably somewhere in their 50's or 60's by this time, and they have kids of their own who are grown and gone. They are making more income than they had made most of their lives and are in a relatively high tax bracket with few deductions. Now you pass away and hand them a load of taxable accounts they have to pay taxes on at their highest income tax rate. If their highest rate is around 30%, your legacy is only worth 70% of what you were hoping. This is one of those times 30% off is a bad thing. Try to leave non-qualified accounts (not annuities) and Roth IRAs to your heirs, so they don't have to think about the taxes and instead think about how you would want them to enjoy these funds.

Of course, this isn't the exact situation for everyone, but most people transition their wealth with some variation of this storyline. They just haven't thought through the full ramifications of leaving taxable accounts to their heirs. There are a couple of other ways to lower the overall taxable legacy to your heirs. Of course, these strategies only work if your tax rate in retirement is lower than your heir's tax rate while still working. Of course, you will want to consult your tax professional before moving ahead with any of these strategies.

Liquidation Strategy
When taking money out of investments to support your lifestyle, use taxable money first. A tax professional can help you liquidate taxable accounts up to a preferred effective tax percentage. Basically, you will take a predetermined amount from your taxable accounts to pay taxes on them at a rate you and your accountant are comfortable with. Any income you need above your agreed upon taxable amount, look to non-taxable assets to take more funds.

Roth Conversions
In the same vein as above, if you do not need the income, convert a portion of your taxable accounts—up to the amount your accountant directs you to pay taxes on— to Roth accounts every year. Ask your accountant what effective tax rate to target, and have them calculate exactly how much to have as earned income to reach that target rate. Your tax professional can then do the math to see how much more you can add to your

current income from your conversions to get there.

Liquidate Gains from Non-qualified Annuities
A non-qualified annuity can be beneficial in your earning years, saving you capital gains taxes on your investment growth. However, someone will have to pay earned income taxes on those gains eventually. If it's not you, it will be your beneficiaries. You may be better off liquidating the gains from these annuities over time to pay the taxes at *your* rates and leave your heirs other assets that have a step-up in cost basis with no taxes to pay on the unrealized gains before death.

Keeping the Family Peace
At this point, you may be asking, "what if I don't care as much about the financial side of the legacy I leave?" If that's the case, you're definitely not alone, and thankfully this book covers your health, too. The most valuable part of your legacy is the memories you leave for those you love. Honestly, what do you know about the person who your local library was named after? Unless it was a U.S. President or a celebrity, do you care? No. However, you've surely heard a story or two about a family who fought over their parents' inheritance and now doesn't even talk to each other. The best thing you can do to help ensure there is no fight over your assets or other wishes is to make your wishes clear; tell your beneficiaries what you want while still alive. There is nothing to be gained from keeping your wishes to yourself.

You can certainly tell your kids or other heirs what you want them to do with the money, but the legal way is to have your estate documents in order. As covered earlier, for your plan protection, there are four documents almost everyone needs:

1. Will,
2. Power of attorney for health,

3. Power of attorney for finances, and
4. Living will.

As previously noted, go to an estate-planning attorney in your state, as each state is a little bit different with regard to the language you need in these documents and the look of your overall plan. If you don't have a large or complicated estate plan or you're willing to do the tedious work of titling each asset appropriately, you may not need a trust to ensure your wishes are met. This is known as a will-based estate plan.

Although it is advisable to create an estate plan for leaving money to your heirs, spend your money. *You earned it. You saved it.* Enjoy it with those you love. Try to leave your heirs more memories than money when all is said and done.

Common Question: Do I need to set up a trust?

There are many different types of trusts, but revocable living trusts for estate planning are the type referenced in the question above. Such a trust does two things for an estate plan: bypass probate to save your loved ones time and money, direct exactly where you want assets to go, and guide when your beneficiaries can access them. Think of it like a bucket that holds what you own, and if you die, the bucket is handed off and your instructions followed.

If you have a large estate, you probably want to set up a trust just to ensure all of your assets are distributed according to your wishes. Wills have to go through the court system known as probate. Trusts, if done correctly, bypass probate and the courts altogether. Assets that go through probate will follow the instructions in your will, but court decisions don't always line up with what you want. There could be a discrepancy in the wording in a will or a dispute among family members of what you may have meant by that wording, and families could fight in court over a will for years. These issues could add time and cost in determining where the funds will go. Do you really want to pay attorneys and depend on a judge to get your preferences right?

You can also avoid probate by designating specific beneficiaries for titled assets and accounts. Those beneficiary designations are followed without going to court. If you do a good job adding Payable on Death (POD) or Transfer on Death (TOD) designations or named beneficiaries to your bank accounts, retirement accounts, real estate, and life insurance, you may be able to avoid probate without the cost of setting up a trust. You just have to be diligent in getting all accounts updated with the correct paperwork. Also, if your wishes change, you have to ensure you update all accounts affected.

You may need a trust if you have a specific worry about one of your beneficiaries and need to spread their inheritance out over time, if you own a business, or own uniquely valuable collections of personal property. If you exceed your taxable estate threshold, you should ask an attorney about irrevocable trusts for tax planning and asset protection.

The most common issue is the need to spread an inheritance over time. Your beneficiary might need a more structured distribution schedule because of age or circumstances. For instance, there may be family members with substance abuse issues; to get their annual distribution from the trusts, these beneficiaries could be required to submit to a drug test. The beneficiaries also could be minor children and ill-equipped to receive a lump sum of money. Many grantors use a trust to space out the allowed income withdrawals over time and ensure their legacy is used how they would see fit or at least not squandered when a young adult heir spends immaturely.

Use a trust-based estate plan when concerned the funds you've spent your life growing and saving will be used for something other than what you had envisioned. Whether used by one of your heirs or Uncle Sam taking a large chunk of it, a trust may be an option. See an estate-planning attorney you trust who can help you evaluate the benefits and drawbacks of the will versus the trust-based plan. Trust-based plans are much more expensive, so void an attorney who tells you a trust is the only way to go without explaining the value for the added cost.

Teach Your Children Wealth Planning

If you have children, part of your legacy will be how your kids live their lives, so begin to teach them how to make sound financial decisions. Most wealthy people will say their parents taught them how to manage money and create good habits around their spending and saving. And most people who aren't as financially well off say their parents did not model positive financial habits or teach them anything about their finances. Typically, those who aren't where they'd like learned financial lessons through trial and error the hard way, and that takes a long time. Almost everyone blames their parents for where they are financially, for better or worse.

Take the time to teach your children good skills, so they speak highly of you and keep your legacy intact. You can hand your kids a book like this one. Talk to them about all the lessons and information covered, and your kids will be better educated than most Americans. However, the best thing you can do for your kids is to model the lessons. Do what is necessary to be where you want to be financially and discuss your decisions with them. Talk to your kids about why you're buying a used car versus the shiny new one on the lot. Review your decision to buy a new laptop with them. You could talk about what considerations are important and not important to you when shopping for a laptop. Tell them what you're willing to pay for and what you don't need to spend money on. You can even model in the grocery store by explaining why you decided to buy organic milk even though it costs more. If you choose not to buy organic, explain to your kids how you made that decision when evaluating the costs and the benefits. When you include your children in the financial conversations, you'll pass along your values. In general, you tell the world what you value through how you spend your time and your money. Your values *are* your legacy.

Periodically review your finances and include your kids when they reach an appropriate age. Discuss future major decisions in family meetings. Let them have an opinion if they want, or just let them watch and listen as you discuss the decision you have to make and the reasoning behind the option you chose. If you'd rather they didn't voice an opinion in the discussion, listen to their opinion afterward and ask questions about how they derived their opinion. Don't make them feel dumb or uncomfortable in the conversation, even if their opinion isn't the best. Use language like "That's interesting, tell me more...Have you considered...? Or I see where you're coming from, but how about this...?" instead of dismissive language that will turn them off from future conversation. The goal isn't necessarily for them to understand the first time; it's to engage them in the process of making a decision, so they learn valuable, life-long decision-making skills.

Say it's time to buy a car, and during the family discussion, you're debating between an older truck and a newer car. You could weigh needing space for kid's sports equipment, resale value, comfort, gasoline consumption, and insurance cost. All of those preferences matter while making a larger purchase decision like a car. Let the kiddos see how you consider a decision of magnitude in a mature manner, so they won't have to make the same mistakes most kids make when they become adults and buy something unnecessary just because they want it. If you can help your kids avoid buying for want instead of need when it comes to large purchases alone, you'll be placing them at the front of the pack with financial education. They'll thank you for it and speak highly about your values for a lifetime to come.

Leaving Your Legacy of Wellness

As you start on your fitness journey, you'll be excited to see personal results and take steps to become healthier. If you're like me, you'll gain even more joy from the fact those close to you at home and work, as well as random acquaintances, will take steps to become healthier as well. They will ask what you're doing to look and feel better, or they'll start acting by osmosis. The lead-by-example approach to fitness leaves a lasting impression on those you influence. You may not realize it at the time, but becoming healthy will lead to a legacy of wellness among those closest to you and even some not as close.

As a teenager, I picked up smoking cigarettes; it's embarrassing to admit being the health nut I am today, but it's true. My girlfriend at the time, now wife, and I decided to quit together after we met. It was a difficult process, but we supported each other and completely stopped cold turkey, as they say. Within a year or so, no one in our immediate families smoked cigarettes anymore. We didn't push anything on them, but we did show it was possible. Our example helped those we love to make better decisions. You will see the same thing once you start seeing results and feeling good.

We all lead by example, positively or negatively. The saying "do what I say, not what I do" does not work. Those you lead may do what you say when you're in the room, but your team will imitate what you do as soon as you leave. Align what you say with what you do for fitness too. Tell your family, friends, and loved ones what you're doing and why you're working hard, making the decisions you're making. They will be inspired to make their own changes, however small they may be.

Teach Your Kids Fitness

My kids know we work out in the morning before they are awake. When I go to wake my son, he often asks me if I've already worked out. Since Dexter was as small as I can remember, he would be with me in the basement doing push-ups. Of course, his push-ups weren't proper form all the way to the ground with elbows at 90 degrees and his butt in line with his back, but I'm told seven years old is too young to bring that up with him. Apparently, he's too young, and I'm overbearing with unrealistic expectations of a seven-year-old...yeah, yeah...

The key is for your kids to know you value fitness. They will naturally pick up your fitness values and run with them (figuratively and probably literally). You don't have to make protein shakes for them and stand over them while doing push-ups to show your values. All you have to do is talk about your decisions. How do you spend your time? Why do you spend it that way? Remember, people show what they value through where their time and money are spent. Are you spending time making healthy food at lunch, or are you driving through at the fast food place down the road? Your kids are paying attention.

One of the easiest ways to let your kids know you value fitness is to evaluate your time spent together and ensure that time isn't only watching television or eating fast food. Do you go on walks together as a family? Do you let the kids play at the playground and run around with them too? When you help them practice for their sports or other physical activities, are you participating physically with them or sitting on the sidelines?

Many people will say kids shouldn't lift weights before their growth plates have finished growing, or they'll stunt their growth. There is no evidence this is true. You don't need to start your kids with dumbbells and barbells before high school. They can do push-ups, pull-ups, lunges, squats, band work, and other, safer resistance training. The reason for waiting on the weights is more fine-motor-skill related than anything else. You want your little ones to have complete control over their body's movements before lifting heavy weights, or you could risk their injury more than necessary. Their bodies already have weight and provide more than enough resistance for them.

Another legacy to leave for your kids is a positive body image. As children, we watched our parents and idolized them at times. If you are standing in front of the mirror, complaining about how you look, you are teaching your children that it's okay to dislike the way you look. Genetically, they will probably end up looking a lot like you, so set an example of loving yourself as you are and improving your body through fitness because you *love yourself*, not because you dislike something about yourself. Keep in mind, body image affects boys as much as girls, so pay attention to your subtle cues and help them learn positivity around their bodies as they grow up.

If you have children and leave them with a fitness value, your legacy will span generations. More than likely, your healthy values will pass from your kids to your grandchildren, and so on. If you want to impact the future of your family positively, leave a legacy of fitness.

Leaving a legacy in health and wealth is about making positive choices for yourself and ensuring your kids are involved in the decision-making process, so they understand not just what you chose but why you made that choice. Kids are observant, intuitive, and smart. They are picking up on everything you do, whether you realize it or not. They will even understand your intentions and mindset without knowing what those words mean. Remain mindful they are watching you all the time. Try to make more decisions in line with your goals than decisions against your goals and talk about those decisions. Even talk about the ones you aren't proud of, so your kids hear your reasoning instead of creating it themselves.

Leaving a Financial Legacy	**Leaving a Fitness Legacy**
OK to leave to heirs – Traditional IRA	Lead by Example
Better – Non-Qualified Accounts	Fitness & Food Choices
Best – Roth IRA	Kids Can Wait on Weights
Not so Good – Non-Qualified Annuities	Impart a Positive Body Image
Express wishes with legal estate documents	

Be Healthy Enough to Leave <u>*More Memories Than Money*</u>.

Hiring Professional Help

Can you take care of all this money planning, saving, and investing on your own? Absolutely. Do you want to? Probably not. Hiring a professional to guide you in financial planning and management of your investments can greatly improve your chances of success. An advisor has licenses, training, and experience, so they have likely seen a situation similar to yours many times before. They can help you avoid risks and take advantage of opportunities you would otherwise not know. An advisor can be an unemotional yet involved sounding board. They need to care about your success but not be in the middle of the decision you are making. Financial decisions always have an element of math and an element of emotion, and your advisor can help you navigate the path between the two. Any computer can give you a calculation, but it takes a person with experience to understand what drives your decision to give you the information you need to make one that's right for you.

Hiring a fitness professional or personal trainer is similar to a financial planner. Could you get fit on your own? Of course. Will you? Probably not. A personal trainer is there to help hold you accountable to your specific goals and push you farther than you'd push yourself. They will keep track of your progress and keep you safe by holding you to proper form and spotting you with certain exercises. The decision of who to hire as your trainer is as meaningful as who your financial planner will be. In this chapter, you will find tips to help you choose them both wisely.

> **Common Misconception: You have to be rich to have a plan and a financial planner**
>
> Begin planning your financial life now, like *right* now. Even if you have a mountain of debt and don't have the income to support it, make a plan. If you don't know where to start, please call someone to help. Many advisors have minimum requirements to work with them, but others will work with anyone they feel is motivated to improve their financial life. You don't need a fancy, high-dollar planner to get good advice. Eventually, you may want to hire a fancy planner, but don't worry about that now. Just get started and work the plan.

Hiring a Financial Professional

There are many different types of financial planners out there. You could have an independent advisor who doesn't recommend any of their own company's products or a captive advisor who only represents one company's products. You could find a fiduciary, fee-only advisor who is required by law to work in your best interest. Or you could choose an advisor who has to recommend planning to be suitable for someone in your situation based on vague legal precedence called the "prudent man" rule. In the prudent man rule, the advisor has to prove the recommendation could be viewed as suitable for the client by a "prudent man," whoever that is. There are three types of advisors when it comes to how they charge fees. One of these types is not better than others because you can find an ethical, great planner who is captive and receiving a commission on your products. You could also find an unethical, not-so-great planner who can tout themselves as a fiduciary because of the way they charge fees. As a consumer, you need to be aware of the fees you're being charged and why. Then you can determine if the style is a good fit for what you want from your planner.

How Do Financial Advisors Charge for Services?

Fee-only

When an advisor is fee-only, they will charge you an hourly or annual rate for their services. They don't sell stocks, bonds, mutual funds, or insurance policies, but they will design you a plan and tell you to implement that plan somewhere else. Many consumers like this style of advice, as they know exactly what they are paying for. The downside is, the annual or hourly rate is generally high. These rates can be into the tens of thousands per year or hundreds of dollars per hour. Another downside is the client often has to implement the wonderful plan built for them and determine which products to buy to complete the plan. These plans can have many moving parts, and the portfolio options and insurance available to implement the plan are abundant. Many clients find they are overwhelmed by having to implement their own plan.

Fee-based

A fee-based advisor will charge a fee based on the total funds you have invested with them. Typically, they are paid the same fee no matter which stocks, bonds, mutual funds, or index funds you use in your plan, so a fee-based advisor is motivated to help you reach toward your goals rather than thinking of how much they will be paid on the fund you're purchasing. On the other hand, fee-based advisors may not have access to the same financial tools as other advisors. Some products are only structured as commission-based because that's the only way the underlying math works to make these options viable for the issuing companies. A fee-based advisor would not be able to recommend these products, limiting the scope of your options.

Commission

An independent or captive advisor who works on commission will charge some combination of up-front, back-end, or annual internal fees to sell a product. Independent advisors who use commission-based products have many potential options to support their clients in reaching their goals. Many insurance products, like annuities, are commission-based products. Although many people believe annuities are bad, they have a place in financial planning for specific client situations where guarantees are warranted and worth paying the high fees. Many of these commissionable financial tools have high internal fees that are only disclosed in a cumbersome prospectus few clients actually read because they are thick packets of legalese with the pertinent fee information buried somewhere in the middle. As consumers, feel comfortable asking the advisor what they will be paid for the product they sell. You can decide for yourself if the product and the advisor are worth it.

What Is Their Area of Expertise?

Most advisors work most often in their niche area of expertise. Some advisors focus on asset management and the growth phase of financial planning. Other advisors will focus on the income phase of planning and how to turn those funds you worked your entire life to save into an income plan you can utilize to maintain your lifestyle throughout retirement. Others still will focus on military personnel, single moms, a specific company's retirees, or any number of other focused markets. It's okay to ask where an advisor focuses most of their business to ensure your needs align with their specialty.

What Type of Advice Do They Offer?

The other way to evaluate your advisor is by the type of advice they give. Are they focused on your habits, the plan, the investments and insurance tools, or several of these areas? If you're looking for someone to hold you accountable, hire an advisor who focuses on coaching. If you just need better product recommendations and a review phone call once in a while, someone focused on product tools will suffice. If you want answers to long-term planning questions (like "what if I want to retire at 62 instead of 65?" or "what if I have a long-term care advanced medical event, will I run out of money?"), then you want to choose an advisor who is planning-oriented.

While you could ask a whole list of interview questions to a potential planner, the answers to the following two questions will give you most of the information you need to evaluate if the advisor is for you:

1. How do you get paid?
2. What is the best way for me to reach my long-term goals?

The first answer will be one or multiple of the three fee structures outlined prior. The second answer will clue you in to their approach. They will discuss accountability, decisions, and habits if they are focused on coaching. They will talk about having and sticking to a long-term plan if they are a planner. Finally, they will consider the financial tools for your situation if they are product-based. If you're not sure what advice they focus on, feel free to ask: habits, planning, or products? If they don't have an answer or answer in a way that isn't in line with what you need as a client, find a different advisor.

Do You Like Them?

Although how you're paying an advisor and what you're paying them to do for you are viable considerations, another decision point is compatibility; you must like your financial advisor. If you don't get along, you'll avoid meeting with them, and ideally, you will be meeting with your advisor for years to come. Also, if you don't like your advisor, they probably don't like you either. If your advisor doesn't like you, they won't take good care of you. When I'm excited to see a client and authentically care about what's happening in their life, I'm more engaged and do a better job. My clients have become more like friends and family over the years than mere meetings on my calendar.

The fact of the matter is I am completely biased; everyone benefits from a financial advisor—an outside, professional perspective without the emotions and biases of living in their client's financial life—to help them make decisions. Making financial choices are both mathematically and emotionally charged and are difficult decisions to navigate. They are difficult even when you do this for a living and know what you would recommend to a client in the same situation. My wife and I meet regularly with a colleague advisor to keep us on track and hold us accountable for decisions that could derail our goals. I can do all of my own math; I know the risks, and I've worked with enough clients to know the pitfalls. Even I do harebrained things every once in a while, as my emotions get in the way. Those are the times advisors truly earn their fees.

Hiring a Fitness Professional

Evaluating a trainer and knowing a good one from a mediocre or bad one is just as difficult as evaluating a financial planner. The advice in the gym between two different trainers can be similar, but a strong trainer will discuss what you're doing outside the walls of the facility they're in. Without strong accountability for habits outside the gym, you'll never reach your goals. The baseline criteria for your decision to hire a trainer is how they discuss what you do outside of their training hours. If they're not interested in anything but the workout you pay them for, find someone else. Once you have the baseline established, you can differentiate between trainers by their certifications, specialties, availability, and personality.

Is the Trainer Certified by a Reputable Company?

There are many certification companies out there. You'll want a trainer certified by a company with an upstanding reputation that puts trainers through a proper fitness curriculum instead of an easy test merely for show. You can ask your prospective trainer who certified them and then research the company's website and their certification requirements. You're looking for certifications that require their candidates to complete actual classes around fitness topics like flexibility, safety with form and spotting, monitoring and tracking results, anatomy, etc. Some designations out there just have a list of practice questions and a test. Designations without classes attached to them are a breeze for someone good at test-taking; these programs are ineffective for most. You can also find out if they need continuing education to maintain their certification. While continuing education can seem like a bureaucratic hoop to jump through, in a profession like fitness where the science is continuously challenged and updated, ongoing education is essential. Type the designation into a search bar. You will find their governing bodies and be able to see the conditions to achieve the designation as well as the continuing education requirements.

What Is Their Specialty?
Again, you will want to ensure your prospective trainer's area of expertise meets the needs you have as a client. If you're looking for overall health and wellness, a trainer with a certification in powerlifting probably isn't right for you. If you want to gain size and bench press a small car, then a yoga instructor is not a good fit. While researching the certification body, investigate the specialty the organization values and stresses in their training. Chances are your trainer will follow their lead. You can find certifications specializing in sports injury rehabilitation, flexibility and mobility, and nutrition, among many others.

Are They Easy to Get To?
Convenience is a priority. Going out of your way will end in either not going to your sessions or not scheduling them in the first place. If you're

not meeting your trainer often enough, you might as well not have one at all. Many trainers have their own gyms, will come to your home and use your equipment, or work inside a big gym where you're already a member. Nowadays, there are even plenty of trainers offering digital sessions over teleconference. Find a trainer easy to get to amid the hustle and bustle of your life and your schedule.

Can They Meet with You Often?
Plan to see your trainer regularly. Prospective clients often ask trainers to develop a workout they can repeat all month and then return for a new workout the next month. The loose regimen doesn't work as a client's lifestyle generates change. Working out is less than half of the battle, and you can find workouts online for free if that's all you need. If you see your trainer at least weekly, you will tell them what you're eating, the workouts you're doing, and how they make your body feel. The habits you cultivate outside the gym are more relevant to your health than the fitness and strength you form inside the gym. Your trainer can help you determine the outside influences holding you back and help change your habits to break through the plateaus and reach your goals. They can only provide this value if you meet regularly. Obviously, it is more expensive to hire a trainer weekly or even bi-weekly. Would you rather pay more for results or pay less for wasted time and effort?

Do You Like Them?
Similar to your financial planner, make sure you like your personal trainer. You will be talking to this person at least weekly, and you'll be sharing intimate parts of your life with them—like your diet and sleep habits—to ensure they have the information they need to help you make healthy decisions. They will pinch your fat and tell you hard things such as "you're putting in the work in the gym, but you're not fol-

lowing through on your commitments to yourself outside of the gym." Sometimes clients will break down and cry in discussions like this as their insecurities and fears are front and center. You'll want to like your trainer when you have these honest conversations. If you're uncomfortable with your trainer or just not looking forward to your sessions, you will be more likely to cancel or not show up. That doesn't do you any good. You'll also want to make friendly small talk between sets, maybe even throw them a few wisecracks, like telling your trainer you think they're enjoying your pain a bit too much. (they are likely enjoying your pain a little bit) If you are spending an hour a week or more with this person, you deserve to enjoy the conversation.

Professional advice will help you reach your goals faster and more effectively than learning and doing everything independently. Even though you have access to all the information you need—in books, courses, and online—to get healthy and wealthy, having someone holding you accountable to reach your goals is typically worth it.

Hiring a Financial Professional	**Hiring a Fitness Professional**
Fees – Fee-Only, Fee-Based, Commission?	Certifications from a Reputable Company?
Area of Expertise?	Area of Expertise?
Type of Advice – Habit, Plan, Products?	Easy to Get To? If not, you won't go.
How often do you meet? Quarterly, annually?	How often do you meet? 1,2,3x per week?
Do you like them?	Do you like them?

At this point, you have the mindset, the plan, and the habits. You have the basis of education necessary to improve your life in both health and wealth. Now let's look at how you can use the time to create the life you have always wanted.

The next section will cover the different life phases and the challenges one might find in each phase. Also covered are the areas of health and wealth you will want to focus on while in specific phases of life.

LIFE PHASES

Getting Started

You made it. You're an adult, and you are off to become your own person. In the Getting Started phase of life, you may have a job or three, but most haven't found their career just yet. You're learning how much supporting your life actually costs with health insurance, cell phone bills, car payments, etc. You're making decisions about school loans and other debt. You have a lot of room for error at this stage of your life, but with some diligence and learning from others' mistakes, you can avoid some of the errors and get ahead of success sooner in life. Many can eat pizza every day in this life phase and still stay fit so long as you work out regularly. Believe me. I lived this. You could also pay more than necessary for a car you want but don't need and end up with it in the shop more than you get to drive it, all the while flushing money down the drain. Admittedly, I lived this, too.

Common Question: Should I buy or rent?

This is not really a math question. Can you leverage your dollars by taking a mortgage and allowing your equity to multiply without investing as much capital as you would with another investment? Yes. But buying a home and selling it within five years means you're mostly paying interest on an amortized loan. Amortization front-loads most of your interest, so most of your first several years of payments go toward interest and most of your last few years toward principal. This means the typical American way of life, moving or refinancing every five years, keeps us paying interest most of the time. The interest rate the mortgage broker quoted is the compounded interest added to the loan amount based on the current loan value. Throughout the loan, you will pay far more in interest payments than the quoted percentage. Let's look at a $100,000 mortgage with a rate of 5% for 30 years. Your principal and interest payments are $536.82.

# of years	Total Amount Paid	Mortgage Balance	Principal Paid	Interest Paid (% of payments toward interest)
5	$32,209.20	$91,828.73	$8,171.27	$24,038.03 (74.6%)
10	$64,418.40	$81,342.07	$18,657.93	$45,760.66 (71.0%)
20	128,836.80	$50,612.28	$49,387.72	$79,449.46 (61.7%)
30	193,255.20	$0.00	$100,000	$93,255.20 (48.24%)

If you move after the first five years, you'll have paid 74.6% of your payments toward interest. You may get some growth in value on your home, but that's a risk. It feels good to buy because you have the feeling of being able to own something and improve it to add value to your bottom line. However, unless you're in a booming housing market that's increasing at breakneck speed, you pay for most of the typical growth in value the first few years you're in a home through interest on your mortgage. It is also possible to lose value on a home as well, and sometimes, you could lose enough value where the home could not be sold for as much as you owe. In these cases, it makes moving and changing direction in your life far more difficult and costly for your future. Anyone telling you that renting is like putting money in a paper bag and lighting it on fire is either uneducated or, more likely, selling you a property or a mortgage.

Renting is a lifestyle decision that will not add value to your net worth, but leasing does come with its own intrinsic value. You can pick up and move relatively quickly. If you are looking for a job and willing to take one anywhere in the country, don't buy right now. Depending on where you live, it could be cheaper to rent as well. Your cash flow could benefit from renting for a few years in an area where it's expensive to own a home. Also, you don't typically have to worry about repairs or anything else while renting. If something breaks, you call the landlord, and they are responsible for fixing it. The landlord is responsible for the maintenance in most situations as well. Again, the decision to rent is only partially a math decision. Mostly, it is a lifestyle choice. If you're up in the air, rent. If you're ready to commit to one place, buy. And of course, if you want numbers run for your specific information, call a planner.

Most people don't contribute to their retirement plans, work out, or really think about their future much at all during the Getting Started phase of life. That's okay, but not advised. The best thing you can do for yourself when just getting started is just that: *get started.* Begin the habits that will carry you through the rest of your life. You may not be able to save much, but if you start investing $25 or $50 per paycheck into a retirement account, it won't even be a question whether or not to contribute when you're making decent money. Get used to setting aside a portion of your income, so you don't fall into the goldfish trap of increasing income, increasing lifestyle, and wake up much later in life with nothing saved. Build that foundation right away. Another added benefit is compound interest grows when someone starts early. Here's another perspective:

How much to save monthly to get to $1 Million by age 65 with 7% growth

Starting Age	Monthly Savings Required	Total Amount Invested to age 65
20	$263.67	$142,381.80
30	$555.23	$233,196.60
40	$1,234.46	$370,337.59
50	$3,154.95	$567,890.89

If that doesn't get you excited to start saving early, nothing will.

Stay active after high school. There are many examples of people taking an extended break from physical activity after organized sports, becoming overweight by 30 pounds or more, and their hearts and lungs are not as trained as they used to be. Now they're trying to get back in shape, and the physical aspects are one thing, but the mental aspects are entirely another. These men and women were athletes, and they want to train as if they are still in competition shape. If you let yourself get out of shape (and out of the habit) for that much time, your mind will want to push as hard as you used to, but your body will not allow it. That can be demoralizing and difficult to overcome when starting with fitness again.

As with your finances, the best health plan is to stay on track or at least get started now and not start from scratch later. In the Getting Started phase of fitness, it is easy to think you're going to feel good forever. Your joints feel good, you can run when you need to without pulling a muscle or otherwise hurting yourself, and daily tasks are manageable. The problem is that feeling of everything being physically easy to do doesn't last forever. The degradation of physical health happens at a much slower rate if you're working on your fitness throughout your earlier life stage. Join a club team, go to the gym regularly, or at least head outside for a walk or run a few times a week. You don't have to go crazy at this stage, but the better shape you're in before the next stage of life, the easier that stage will be. If you need the extra motivation, sign up for an obstacle race, triathlon, fun run, or whatever challenge keeps you moving.

You have a lot of room for mistakes in the early years; time is on your side. You can eat an entire box of sugary cereal with a half-gallon of whole milk while binge-watching your favorite show most days and still stay reasonably healthy so long as you work out. Regardless, you'll want to start and keep the good habits of regular improvement for your health and wealth throughout this phase of life. Although the typical person getting started doesn't have a lot of discretionary income to do whatever they'd like, starting a savings plan with a small amount can make a big difference in the long run. Remember, the key to all health and wealth is to make more goal-oriented decisions than not over a long period.

Tips for Getting Started

- ❏ Move in a positive direction with your fitness in finances and health–don't worry about having rock-solid goals. You don't need them.

- ❏ Start saving – Time is your biggest asset at this stage due to compound interest
  - ○ *Emergency fund*
  - ○ *Roth IRA*
  - ○ *Individual non-qualified investment account*
- ❏ Apply for life insurance (permanent is preferable) – Easier to get and cheaper to have when you're young.
- ❏ Be active doing what you love–team sports, running, swimming, skiing, surfing, racquetball, etc.
- ❏ Develop the habits now, so you can maintain them when it counts.

Mid-Career

As you reach mid-career, you moved beyond the jobs of the past and into something of a professional career. You will have made or will be making some big life decisions: sharing your life with someone, buying a house, having kids and saving for their college, paying down debts, vacation plans, etc. This phase of your life isn't as much about an age as it is a perspective. As you are making some of these adulting decisions, you're in the mid-career phase of life.

You don't have as much room for error in your mid-career as you did in the getting started phase. However, you still have a decent amount of time if missteps are made. If you buy a house with a high-interest rate, buy a car you can't afford, or pay down all of your debts—even the low-interest ones—before saving a dime for your future, you could impact your long-term savings in a big way. If you've made a mistake in your financial life, don't worry. You can sell the car, refinance the debt, or start saving now to get back on track. You don't have to be perfect; you just have to make progress. Place one foot in front of the other, and don't let the fact you made a mistake keep you from getting back on track.

If you have developed saving habits as a young adult, continue those habits and increase your savings amounts as your income increases. Keep on keepin' on as they say. Each personal financial situation is different as far as the debt payments, credit score management, savings, etc., that you could confront in this phase of life, so again, have a plan and work your plan.

If you haven't been saving up to this point, you're not screwed. Many Americans in their 30's and 40's say they feel behind because they know they *"should"* have been saving this whole time. If this resonates with you, there are still 15, 20, or more years until reaching retirement age. Start now; it's not too late. Use the resources in this book and online, or find a trusted advisor who can help you navigate the decisions you need to make and tailor them to your specific situation. You'll be okay.

Common Question: 15- or 30-year mortgage?

Unless there is a huge interest rate difference, take a 30-year mortgage and pay it faster if you can. Here's an example:

$200,000 mortgage
30-year rate - 5%
30-year payment - $1,073.65 per month
Interest paid over 30 years - $186,511.59

15-year rate - 4.5%
15-year payment - $1,529.99 per month
Interest paid over 15 years - $75,397.58

The 15-year has a compelling story when it comes to the math, right?

What if we paid the 15-year payment on the 30-year loan?
- Time it takes to pay off the loan? 15 years, 9 months
- Total interest paid over that time? $89,485.36

Yes, you would pay an extra $14,000-and-change in interest over the 15-year loan, but you would have more options. If the 15-year mortgage payment is a bit of a stretch or anything happens to your cash flow, such as temporary unemployment, you may have to restructure the loan to meet your needs at an ill-advised time. With the 30-year mortgage, just personally adjust your payment to the agreed-upon-terms until you are in a viable position to send the additional monies. Leave yourself options; locking into a higher payment will probably save you some money over time, but it will also lock you into a future you may or may not have. Life can change a lot in 15 to 30 years, and you need the flexibility to change with it.

It is easy to lose the plot in mid-career with your health. You have family, career aspirations, a social life, and a whole host of other things pulling you in every direction, but you cannot let your health suffer. If you don't take the time to remain healthy, you won't have as much energy or confidence to keep up with the increasing demands on your time and energy. The workouts may have to be completed in less time because you can't spend the entire afternoon in the gym anymore, but you need to keep doing what you can when you can. The workout types may need to change as well. You probably won't get the same results from walking into the gym, throwing some weight around, and getting in your car to head home as you did in your twenties. You'll want to incorporate more cardio for your heart and stretching to get out of bed the next day without a ton of pain. Your food intake has a greater impact during this phase of life, as well. You'll start noticing a couple of beers every night of the week will lead to a gut and a sluggish feeling halfway through your day. The lack of nutritious fuel is noticeable at this age, so pay attention to your food intake and shoot for high protein, high fiber, low sugar, and low saturated fat.

Another major health concern in mid-career is stress. Stress creeps up on us in mid-career. Take a few minutes each day for some intentional breathing, introspection, and mindfulness. The effect of stress on the body is so bad it has been compared to smoking five cigarettes per day, and all it takes to combat is some self-awareness and a few minutes for yourself. If you feel the effects of stress creeping up on you, do what your mind and body need to relieve that stress. That way, you can keep the long-term adverse effects of stress at bay.

Your workouts may have to change in more ways than duration. Many my age have dealt with surgeries, injuries, or illnesses that make working out the way they did in the past impossible. If you find yourself in this category during mid-career, it's time to get creative. If your ankles lost all their cartilage because you ran cross country in high school and consistently wore down your joints, it's time to learn to ride a bike, hike the stair stepper, or row the rower. You may not enjoy these new activities as much as what you used to do but find activities that hold your attention and get to work. You could try swimming or Zumba; it doesn't matter what exercise you choose as long it gets you moving. Keep resistance training in your routine as well. Muscle loss due to age begins in your 30's. Most don't feel the effects for a while but maintaining your resistance training will fight that loss as it starts. You may have to move to machines or bands rather than benches, bars, and dumbbells, and that is perfectly okay. Whatever you do, don't give up on yourself just because you have to change how you stay in shape.

If you do the hard work in health and wealth during this phase of your life —as your kids age, as you settle into your career, and other demands settle down a bit—you'll definitely be set up for success in your future. If you haven't even started yet, you still have time to get going, but the window is closing. Instead of adjusting your expectations for your future, get going on your savings now.

Tips for Mid-Career
- Progress is important; perfection is not.
- Work out for more energy, not to deplete it.
  - *Cardio for heart strength.*
  - *Resistance training to maintain muscle and bone density.*
- Increase your savings as your income increases:
  - *401k,*
  - *Possibly more life insurance needs,*
  - *529's for college planning.*
- Add fun life goals.
  - *Fitness–Bucket list items–i.e., complete an Ironman race, climb Mount Kilimanjaro, run a marathon, etc.*
  - *Finance–i.e., college funding, vacation homes, financial freedom, etc.*

Pre-Retirement

In the pre-retirement phase of life, your kids are typically either teenagers who do not want to be around you or a bit older, and they've already left the nest for their own adventure. You're likely making decent money with the least non-discretionary expenses you've had in a while since those kids, who could eat you out of house and home, are on their own—that's why these are called your golden years. You will probably be able to save quite a bit of your income at this point. The typical American is looking at their lacking retirement account around this phase, thinking, "I should really start thinking about my future." If this is you, and this is most people, then it's likely you're going to have to work a little while longer than your early 60's. Don't worry, though. Many people think they will retire at a certain age, but they end up working longer because 60 doesn't seem as old as they thought it did before they arrived. Even if someone could easily retire monetarily in their early 60's, many work into their 70's anyway. Most who do say something like, "I didn't know what I'd do with myself if I didn't work." Hopefully, you're well on your way to financial independence by now, and all we have to do is fill in the gaps in the home stretch.

Now is the time to start repositioning all the growth-oriented assets you've spent your working years cultivating into your income-oriented plan. You really can't take the full risk of the market anymore. If a great recession hit and you lost 50% of your investments, you'd have to continue working a while longer. We don't want that, so let's start the reduction of risk now. At this phase of life, think of risk as a dimmer switch rather than a light switch. We want to lower the risk in your portfolios by moving stock investments to more bonds or other low-risk vehicles, as you are closer to a realistic retirement time frame. Even if you choose to work after you no longer *have* to—that choice is retirement—your investments need to be allocated accordingly.

Common Question: Are annuities bad?

An annuity is an insurance product that provides an investment feel. The products can provide a fixed return like a CD, an indexed return that references one of the indices but does not directly invest in it, or a variable return that actually invests in a market-driven product similar to a mutual fund. These products add a level of protection to your investments. Annuities are typically expensive and complicated because clients have to pay for the added protection of the insurance. These products will guarantee a growth rate, withdrawal rate, or both. Benefits like these can be expensive for the consumer if the insurance company is taking all the risk for loss of investment. The insurance company will want to be compensated for the added risk. When the situation calls for it, an annuity can be the solution you're looking for, but the parameters have to be just right.

When someone is within ten years of retirement, and they are unsure their assets will be enough to carry them through the rest of their life at a comfortable income, an annuity could bridge the gap and help the pre-retiree sleep better at night knowing, at a minimum, they will have a certain income based on the insurance benefits of the annuity they purchased. It's essential to only use annuities for a portion (usually less than half) of your liquid net worth as they are most often illiquid vehicles, meaning you can't easily change the purpose of the financial vehicle when your life plan changes. Having other assets in more liquid financial instruments will ensure you're flexible when a change is warranted.

You'll also want to prepare your future income strategy. While all conversions from growth to income are a bit different, you'll want to convert your assets in a way your income keeps up with your cost of living throughout your life. You also need to set aside assets or purchase insurance to protect yourself against advanced medical care in the long run. Most people will also want to protect their future by reducing their "have to" expenses. To do this, you could pay off some or all of your outstanding debt to reduce your fixed-income need during your upcoming retirement. Then you can stockpile fun money to do some traveling or whatever it is you want to spend your discretionary funds on. Another popular option to reduce the income need in retirement is downsizing your home. Depending on the real estate market at the time of sale, trading your large, expensive home for a smaller, less expensive one could be a viable option for reducing expenses. The earlier you set your fixed income with cost reduction, inflation protection, and advanced medical costs in mind, the more you can fund the fun money area of your income strategy. All kinds of products can help with setting up this income game-plan. Speak with your trusted advisor to help produce a plan for you and ensure they show how your strategies will protect your lifestyle from inflation over the long term, market risk in the short term, and the possibility of advanced medical costs in your future.

At this stage of your life, fitness becomes far less about looking good and much more about feeling good…although you're still going to look good. You need to maintain resistance training in your routine as weightlifting can increase bone density to fight future osteoporosis and loss of testosterone, which is a vital hormone for both sexes. Although you still need to lift some weight, more reps with lighter weight will suffice for most people in the pre-retirement phase of life. It's a good idea to incorporate some yoga or Pilates, as well. As we age, our balance and flexibility will deteriorate. If you maintain good balance, flexibility, and core strength in pre-retirement, you could slow or even reverse the deterioration of both balance and flexibility, which will keep you more mobile.

If you can remain mobile with healthy bones and the strength to do the things you want to do, you will get a lot more out of your fun money and, arguably, your life. Your travel is far more enjoyable when you're healthy. Too many retirees stop traveling before they really wanted to. It is too difficult to walk around foreign towns, sit on planes, and maneuver their bodies as they needed to get through the airport carrying bags, traversing crowds, or hurrying to make a connection. While you're hopefully saving more than you ever have, focus on your fitness with the same level of intensity. If you can do both at this point in your life, you are setting yourself up for the best kind of retirement, healthy and wealthy.

Tips for Pre-Retirement

- ❏ Prepare now by asking yourself:
  - ○ *Where do you eventually want to live as you transition into retirement?*
  - ○ *What passion or hobby will fill your time? i.e., travel, woodworking, volunteering, side gig as a yoga instructor, etc.*

- ❏ Dimmer switch–Begin de-risking your portfolios a bit every year.
- ❏ Set up your future income strategy.
- ❏ Resistance training–prevents osteoporosis and loss of testosterone.
- ❏ Incorporate yoga and Pilates if you haven't–core, balance, and flexibility.

Retirement

Look at that. You blinked, and now it's time to retire. You can sit around the house, sipping your tea into the winter of your life—not really. Most retirees say, "I don't know where I had the time to get all this done when I was working 40 hours a week." Retirement looks different to everyone, but this phase of life is when you don't *have* to go to work anymore. Some people choose to work well past the time they don't need to because they enjoy their work or can't imagine themselves not working. That's great. Whether you're working in the same career, transitioning into volunteer work, supporting your family, or focusing on your hobbies, the point is you get to choose how you spend your time in the retirement phase.

At this point in your life, most people realize they've spent a lifetime accumulating experience, knowledge, and assets but have no clue what to do with them. Create a plan for how you will use your experience and knowledge with the time you have in retirement. If you haven't created your income plan during pre-retirement, now is definitely the time. Focus on what you want your money to accomplish for you. You'll need some of your money for your day-to-day lifestyle. You'll need to reserve some for future expenses like your next cars, vacations, classes, or any number of other things. Some money you will use to offset future inflation and possible medical needs as you age. Decide now which money is set aside for what and how you intend to use it.

There will be tax implications for different sources of funds. For instance, you will pay earned income taxes on a Traditional retirement account withdrawal and wouldn't on a non-qualified account, so consider these impacts before withdrawing funds. Consult with a tax professional to come up with a tax strategy for today and the future. Rarely do you want to pull all your money from one type of account at a time. Usually, you'll be pulling some from the taxable and non-taxable accounts throughout the year to keep your taxable income within an appropriate agreed-upon range. Your accountant can help you with proforma tax statements to estimate your future tax payments based on different withdrawal strategies. If you are in a lower tax bracket in your 60's, it may make sense to take a bit more from your taxable accounts to lower your future withdrawal amounts and give you more control over your tax consequences.

Common Question: How are retirement accounts taxed?

The **Traditional retirement** account is the one everyone is used to. You get a tax deduction for funds going into the account. Let's take the example that you make $50,000 a year, and you contribute $5,000 to your retirement account that same year. The government will tax you on $45,000 as if you never made that extra $5,000. The $5,000 you contributed will grow tax-deferred in future years, so you also won't have to pay taxes on the growth in the years the funds are growing. However, you will have to pay taxes on every dollar you pull from your Traditional retirement account at the time of withdrawal. Suppose you pull funds before turning 59.5 years old. In that case, you will pay earned-income taxes on the amount withdrawn, as well as a penalty for early withdrawal—barring a few exceptions like disability, higher education, or an IRS levy. On the flip side, tax deferral benefits in a Traditional retirement account have an expiration date. If you still have assets in a Traditional retirement account after you turn 72 years old, the IRS will force you to take money out of your accounts and pay taxes because Uncle Sam hasn't been paid on those assets just yet. IRS rules only require you to withdraw a small percentage to start, but your required minimum distributions increase as a percentage every year until you're taking more than half per year out of the account. You don't necessarily have to use the money to buy anything—the government doesn't care what you use it for—but you cannot leave it in a tax-deferred account.

The **Roth retirement** account has the opposite benefits. You will pay taxes on the earned income the year you make your money and invest in the Roth account. In the example above, even though you contributed $5,000 to your retirement, you will be taxed on the full $50,000. However, the assets do have the same tax deferral as the Traditional retirement account, so you don't pay taxes year to year as the account grows. As long as you've had the account for more than five years and you're over 59.5 years old, you won't have to pay any taxes on the growth in the Roth account. Ever again. You also never have to take funds out of the account because the IRS has already been paid.

If you have set up your income plan appropriately, your income and investments will mostly be on autopilot for a while. Just focus on keeping your plan easy and straightforward. If your plan is too complicated with several accounts at different companies with different tax implications, you could confuse yourself and make a mistake with some significant consequences. Keep your plan simple by knowing what accounts are for what purpose and using investment vehicles with rules that are easy to understand and follow. For instance, if you take money out of an annuity product at a higher rate than you're supposed to or at the wrong time, you could negatively alter the income benefits for life. It has also been my experience one partner will typically know the finances better than the other in a relationship. The more knowledgeable partner doesn't get to make all the decisions, but one partner is generally more in tune with the whole plan. If the more in tune partner passes away first, a complicated plan can cause many issues. High stress with the passing of your partner and the lack of knowledge in products and plans can cause mistakes that cannot be undone, like closing a retirement account and paying taxes on the full account in one year or closing out a unit investment trust too early and having to pay a back end sales charge. Keep the plan simple and discuss your income plan with your partner, including how the money will be used at each retirement stage.

You might find it beneficial to name the accounts as the funds will be used. For example, name the account your monthly income comes from the "Income Account." The money you utilize for trips and unexpected costs could be your "Freedom Account. And your riskier money set aside for the long term could be your "Inflation/Long-Term Account." You'll remember these account names better than the products or portfolios themselves. If you have an advisor helping with your retirement planning, make sure your partner has met them and also feels comfortable with their style—just in case your partner has to call the shots one day. Also, make your advisor's contact information easily accessible, somewhere other than your phone, so an heir could quickly find it if something happened to you. It's awful to learn of a client's death as an advisor, but it is made exponentially better if their spouse or heir has met the advisor in advance.

In retirement, your fitness plays as key a role as your income gameplan. You'll want to ensure your doctor is on the same page you are *before* you work out. Once you get the green light, utilize weightlifting or resistance training to maintain the bone density you're losing over time. Balance, flexibility, and core work are vital at this stage. The societal norm out there is thinking older people lose mobility and often fall; that's just not true. Older adults who don't take care of themselves lose flexibility and mobility—they fall. If you don't use it, you lose it. Sure, unavoidable issues like arthritis or cancer could crop up in the later phase of life, but don't get discouraged and give up. You need to do something for your health every day, no matter how small. If you start to think, "It hurts for me to get up, so I'm just going to stay down," you'll lose all mobility faster than you realize. Keep working on your mobility, flexibility, and balance. The body is resilient and can heal itself, even as we age.

Tips for Retirement

- Simplicity is key.
- Transition fully to your income plan.
- Share your financial plan with your family and heirs.
- Fitness–Keep your doctor in the loop.
- Focus on mobility, flexibility, and balance.
- Resistance training–probably more bands and light weights as you age, but don't stop.
- Be fit – both healthy and wealthy!

TOOL KIT

FitFinancial Test™

The FitFinancial Test™ is an online test that can assess your current financial situation based on recommended financial ratios. Enter information about your income, assets, debts, and savings to evaluate your current financial state as well as your future needs. The questions will only take a few minutes to complete, and you will have your comprehensive report and analysis within seconds.

The analysis includes your most relevant financial ratios: emergency funds, debt-to-income, housing debt, consumer debt, savings rate, and retirement calculations. The Certified Financial Planner Board or CFPB provides the recommended guidelines as acceptable levels for the ideal financial situation.

You can take the questionnaire as many times as you like, adjusting your financial information to create different outcomes that answer your "what if" questions. Here are a few examples:

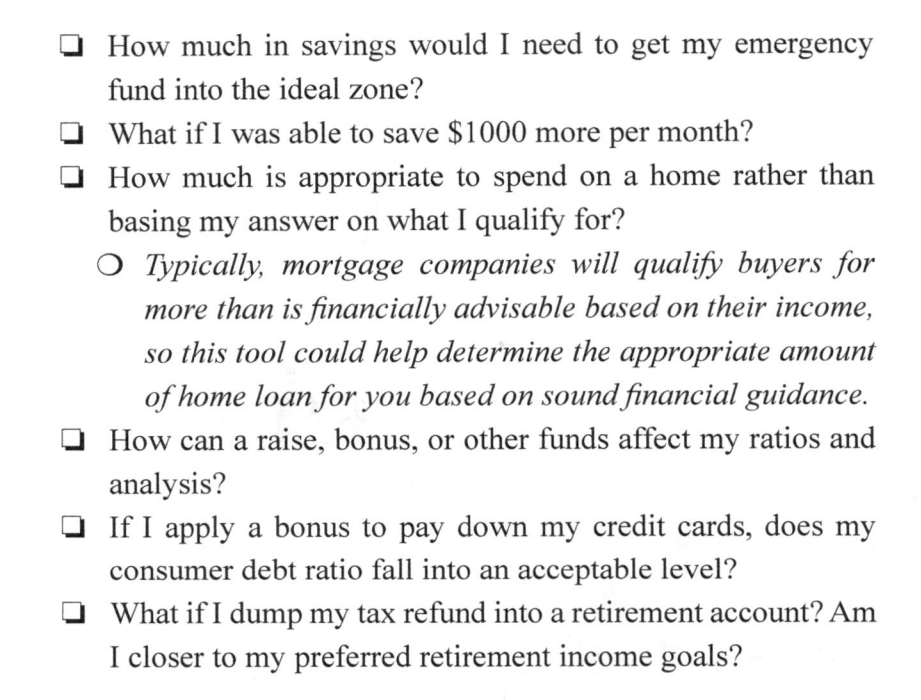

- ❏ How much in savings would I need to get my emergency fund into the ideal zone?
- ❏ What if I was able to save $1000 more per month?
- ❏ How much is appropriate to spend on a home rather than basing my answer on what I qualify for?
  - ○ *Typically, mortgage companies will qualify buyers for more than is financially advisable based on their income, so this tool could help determine the appropriate amount of home loan for you based on sound financial guidance.*
- ❏ How can a raise, bonus, or other funds affect my ratios and analysis?
- ❏ If I apply a bonus to pay down my credit cards, does my consumer debt ratio fall into an acceptable level?
- ❏ What if I dump my tax refund into a retirement account? Am I closer to my preferred retirement income goals?

These are just a few of the questions you can answer using the FitFinancial Test™.

The report and the analysis are an overview calculation based on the inputs of your finances. Financial decisions are made at the intersection of math and emotion, so this report may only be half of the equation. The report is not personalized financial planning advice, but it will give you some thoughts and tips on how to improve your ratios to continue climbing the staircase of progress. Almost everyone could benefit from a tool like the FitFinancial Test™. Who wouldn't like to see where their finances stand in the grand scheme of things? "Am I on track?" is a frequent question. While there really isn't a direct answer to that question, these ratios are a great starting point. If your ratios are outside acceptable levels, your analysis will offer suggestions to bring those ratios closer to the recommendations.

If you have a fundamental question regarding your finances but aren't prepared to call a planner for help, you can use this tool for general guidelines in making your decisions. Once your financial situation has advanced to the point where a basic calculator will no longer answer your questions and provide the insight you need, reach out to a financial planner for guidance.

You can find the FitFinancial Test at www.fitfinancialapproach.com

Quick Fixes

Sometimes shaving off a dollar or two from your monthly budget doesn't feel like it matters, but every dollar counts...always. Sometimes a quick change can make a big difference. It helps to get the ball rolling with some bigger steps. Here are a few quick fixes you could do right away to improve health and wealth.

Try Water First

Our brains will tell us to eat by making us think we are hungry when dehydrated; there is water in most foods. A quick tip: If you feel hungry even though you just ate or still have quite a while before you would typically eat, try drinking a big glass of water and seeing how you feel in a few minutes. This trick also helps right before you sit down to eat a meal. Start your meal by downing a full glass of water. Most people will eat far less than they would have otherwise.

Possible Annual Savings: ***$ on food, lose weight.***

Cut the Cable TV

Most people love to watch a select show every now and again, especially when they can stream it without commercials, but not many people say, "You know...I wish I had more time to watch TV." Most people would be appalled if they knew exactly how many hours per week they sit on their couch watching TV. When they're honest, they don't even really enjoy their TV time. If that's the case, why would you spend $150 a month or more on a premium list of 500 channels when you like roughly two shows you could easily stream or watch on a per-play basis? The cost of buying or renting a season of your favorite show on a video streaming service is low compared to paying monthly for all those channels you never watch. Almost every network now allows you to pay for only their streaming service, so if you like sports, pay for just the sports channel you like. Don't pay for the rugby channel when you can't explain why they pick each other up during a throw-in. I couldn't say why, so I don't pay for the rugby channel. If you do watch TV often, and you like having all 500 options to watch at any given time, no worries. Just call your provider to tell them you're thinking of switching to a cheaper option. They'll likely give you the latest deal. If the deal only lasts for a certain amount of time, set a reminder on the calendar to call them back at that date and repeat the conversation. It works.

*Possible Annual Savings: **$1,620***

Scrap the Landline, Reconsider the Cell Plan

Next, evaluate your phone plan. If you're paying for a home line, you can probably stop. If you're only paying for a landline to get a better deal on TV, read the above section "Cut the Cable" until it sinks in. Is your phone still tied to a fax number? Plenty of services out there allow you to scan and "fax" documents over the Internet. No phone required. You can receive your faxes in the same way, too. (And with the ability to send digital files via encrypted email, who faxes anymore?) Think about how many calls you actually receive on your landline— other than telemarketers? Probably not many, if any, so direct your friends to your cell phone and scrap the landline. As for cell phone plans, most consumers overpay out of convenience. Do you really use all the bells and whistles in your plan? If so, great. Keep doing that. If not, don't pay for them. The many cell service provider companies out there are all tapping into similar networks to provide their service. If you can talk to your friends using the same cellular network with a lesser-known company with cheaper fees, go for it. Only pay more for the premium company providing the network if you have a good reason to. Sometimes the lesser-known company is a better choice.

*Possible Annual Savings: **$600***

Get Honest About Your Gym Membership

Are you using your gym membership? If you're paying $100 per month and going every day, you're paying about $3 per day for your membership. That could be worth it. If you're paying that same $100 per month and go twice a week, you're paying $12.50 per trip. That's probably not as worthwhile. In either case, it's a good idea to assess which equipment and classes you actually use. You can save a ton of money if you join one of the cheaper gyms that just offer cardio, machines, or free weights and cut out the towel service, steam rooms, and group classes. If you like attending fitness or yoga classes, you may be able to pay-as-you-go somewhere else. There's no need to pay for the gym portion just for the gym's sake. Those big gyms only stay open because of the people who pay monthly and rarely go. Don't be one of those people.

*Possible Annual Savings: **$720***

Double Check Subscription Services

Review all of your monthly and annual subscriptions. In this day and age, it is easy—sometimes inadvertently—to sign up for all kinds of services you don't use. You can have a monthly subscription for music, movies, TV, books, credit score updates, domain names, associations, or other services. I even paid for a subscription to a salon that cut my hair once every four weeks and gave me a free cocktail with every service. Typically, I was on the run, so I skipped the drink. I was not getting my money's worth for my subscription because the drink was built into the cost. Go through your bank statements line by line to see what services you're paying for. If you haven't viewed the website or the app in the past month, you may want to reconsider that subscription. Because so many of these expenses are automated, some of them may have gone off your radar, but when you look at your bank statements, you'll see right away if you're paying for an outdated service. You could also look to decrease expenses around these. If you're paying the gold package premium for music, but really you only listen to a station or two while at work, you can find a cheaper option out there.

Possible Annual Savings: $600

Grocery Shopping

Stay in the outer aisles of the grocery store. The packaged goods in the middle are mostly not food. Read the ingredients listed on the boxes. Do those ingredients sound like food? Although not all scientific-sounding ingredients are harmful, many unhealthy ingredients are added to food to modify their shelf life or reduce the presence of bacterial growth, such as sodium nitrate, potassium bromate, monosodium glutamate (MSG), propyl gallate, and the like. The safest thing to do is stay in the aisles where you find fresh produce and whole foods. You can decide whether organic is the way to go for your personal health. Please do your own research and decide for yourself if it matters to you. My editor recommended a book called "Food Rules" by Michael Pollan; it has many sensible ideas on making healthy food choices easier. Take the time to learn to cook with more than a microwave. The price of convenience is high and typically not good for you as the microwavable foods include many chemicals to create a similar flavor to the actual food you could be eating. The microwave has been shown to strip even the good foods of some of their nutritional value. TV dinners are real cheap, and for a good reason, they aren't food.

They are one step above eating plastic. If you want to eat well and for a reasonable price, stick to produce and cook it yourself. Buying a zucchini is less than a dollar right now. You can slice it, lay it on a baking sheet and add salt, pepper, and a drizzle of olive oil. Put it in the oven until it browns on the edges, and you've got a great side for multiple people for less than a dollar. You can do this with broccoli, carrots, cauliflower, sweet potatoes, onions, beets, and more for a cheap and easy side with any dinner. If you're only cooking for two, you can set aside a portion for tomorrow's brown bag lunch (see below).

Possible Annual Savings: $varies & you'll feel better

Brown bag your lunch every day

If you're going out to lunch for a $10 - $15 meal twice a week, that is a $500 to $750 expense every year. Just by packing a sandwich and some snacks, you can save hundreds of dollars. Also, you can prep your meals ahead of time to ensure you're eating healthier options. When we just grab something on the go, most of us make terrible food decisions in the heat of a hunger moment. When you take the time in the morning or the night before to prep your lunch and snacks throughout the day, you won't be prone to rash decisions. Instead, you will be able to check in with your "why" and choose the food that gets you closer to your health goals.

Possible Annual Savings: $500

Quit smoking

Full disclosure, I was a smoker for nearly ten years. It is embarrassing to admit, as I was a health professional at the time. I would train clients in their fitness sessions all day, talking about what it takes to be healthy, then I went home and lit a cigarette. Highly hypocritical, but I did it. Although it was a difficult change, I decided the cost to my health and my wallet was too much, so I quit smoking in December

2009, and I never looked back. Now, when I smell someone else's cigarette smoke, I can't believe I used to do that to myself. Use whatever means you need to quit. Do it for your health. Do it for your cash flow. Do it for your family. Just quit. I used a book by Alan Carr, <u>The Easy Way to Stop Smoking</u>; his way worked for me. The book leaves room for you to change your mindset around the addiction before giving it up, as he does not ask you to stop smoking cigarettes until the end of the book. I needed that time to fully understand the change I was making before fighting the mental part of stopping. Please find what works for you.

*Possible Annual Savings: **$2,292***

Sleep, Sleep, Sleep

Getting more sleep is one of the fastest ways to see a change in your fitness. While you are asleep, your body enters a catabolic state. Catabolic is the opposite of metabolic, where the term metabolism comes from. In a catabolic state, your body repairs itself, building muscle fibers to repair the torn fibers from the daily work of living your life. You also get a chance to recharge your organs and rest your normal bodily functions like your heartbeat and conscious brain. Most Americans do not get enough sleep. Without enough sleep, your body will not repair itself sufficiently, so your body will crave food with protein and fat to help with the repairs. Also, since the brain is not rested, your self-control and discipline are more likely to slip; that doughnut or candy bar will be much harder to resist, and you will likely blow cash on quick purchases you don't really need.

Some of the causes for lack of sleep could include a crazy schedule, too much TV or other forms of blue light before bed, drinking alcohol, pain or some other illness, etc. If you have sleep challenges, make whatever changes necessary to get more of it. The CDC recommends 8-10 hours of sleep per night, but each person will be different.

Listen to your body. If you're not waking up feeling rested, change your life to get more sleep. There are some resources on the website fitfinancialapproach.com you can reference.

Possible Annual Savings: ***It's a wide range of possible amounts***

Drink Less Alcohol

Alcohol stops your sleep cycle in the light sleep stages before getting to the deep, REM (Rapid Eye Movement) sleep. When you drink, the alcohol induces your body to produce adenosine, making you tired and fall asleep faster. The problem is your body wakes up when this fake boost in adenosine wears off, and that typically happens before you get to the full, deep sleep. We have several stages of sleep, and there are different benefits to each stage. In the lighter stages, you can feel refreshed from slowed brainwaves and basically a brain break. This break is why naps can be so helpful throughout your day if you're lucky enough to get the time. Your body recovers during deep sleep, and REM sleep is where the brain flushes toxins. It takes an average of 90 minutes to two hours for adults to get to the REM stage, and you cycle through all of these stages a few times through a night of 8-10 hours of good sleep.

Alcohol also leads to dehydration. Consuming 330ml of beer will generate about 500ml of urine, so you're losing more water than you're taking in. Dehydration is a majority of what causes the hangover feeling the day after too much drinking. It can lead to slower muscle recovery periods and excess soreness from your workouts.

The likelihood you're reaching for the veggie tray while inebriated is quite low as well. Most people make poor food choices when drinking, which leads to needing more good choices to make up for it later.

Your body recovers and improves with water, food, and sleep. Alcohol isn't good for any of those. Please enjoy responsibly if you choose to do so.

Possible Annual Savings: ***$varies & you'll feel better.***

Drink More Water

Water begins and ends this section. It is that important. Drinking enough water can have all kinds of health benefits. Your brain sits in a thick liquid made up of 99% water that protects it. Every cell in your body has water in it, and staying hydrated can keep your skin moisturized throughout the day. Your body needs water to run its essential functions. Dehydration could also lead to overeating. If your body is low on water, your brain may tell your stomach to act hungry, so you will feed it food that also happens to have some water in it. If you notice yourself feeling hungry, it may help to start with a glass of water. If you're still hungry afterward, you may just need a snack, but start with water. Drinking a full glass of water before meals will help curb overeating as well.

The National Academies of Sciences, Engineering, and Medicine have found the recommended daily intake is about 15.5 cups (124 ounces) for men and 11.5 cups (94 ounces) for women per day. These numbers are a good place to start, but the recommended amount changes with size, activity level, overall health, and even the weather. The best rule is the pee test. If your pee is clear or light yellow, you're in the right zone.

Possible Annual Savings: ***$ on food, lose weight.***

CONCLUSION

Travel, do cartwheels, or whatever it is you want to do in life for as long as you can. Having physical and financial fitness can create that for you. If you lack one or the other, you won't have the opportunity for a full life. Don't be fit and broke, or rich and broken. Be both fit and wealthy. You'll have a full life for a long, long time.

If you use the information you have learned and implement the small changes over time that lead to a fit life, you will grow in both your fitness and financial goals in no time. You don't have to be perfect; just keep taking steps for yourself. Do it because you love yourself. Do it because you love your family. Do it for your why, whatever yours may be. You can do it.

The Fit Financial Formula:
[Mindset + Planning + Habits] + Time = Health & Wealth

ABOUT THE AUTHOR

Michael Broker started his life mission to help others live their best lives by obtaining his CPT (Certified Personal Trainer) designation from the National Council on Strength & Fitness and working in the fitness industry. He then transitioned into the financial industry and earned his Certified Financial Planner (CFP®) designation. He is currently the Chief Strategy Officer with Trilogy Financial and serves on the Board of Make-A-Wish Colorado. He has been awarded the prestigious C-Suite Award from the Denver Business Journal but finds the best recognition for his work lies in the satisfaction of the people that he helps and in the time he spends with his family.

COMMON QUESTIONS & MISCONCEPTIONS REFERENCE

Common Questions

How much is 100 calories to eat or burn 8
How much will $100 a month be in 20 years? 10
Where does real estate fit in my portfolio? 89
What percentage do I pay in taxes on the money I make? 99
*How much am I actually paying for something I put
        on a credit card?* 103
Should I pay off my home or invest the money? 106
What do news channels mean by "the market"? 131
Why do I gain weight when I start a workout plan? 139
Why do my knees hurt? 176
Do I need to set up a trust? 184
Should I buy or rent? 202
15- or 30-year mortgage? 207

Are annuities bad? 211
How are retirement accounts taxed? 215

Commonn Misconceptions
Women can get super bulky. 21
Sit-ups will give you abs. 24
You've lost money when the market goes down 38
My home always goes up in value 67
Easy results are not so easy 81
How can I lose the fat on my...? 94
Supplements are key to reaching my fitness goals 111
Gold is safe. 136
I will make up for my lack of sleep on the weekend 147
Social Security isn't going to be there for me 156
You have to be rich to have a plan and a financial planner 192

A free ebook edition is available with the purchase of this book.

To claim your free ebook edition:
1. Visit MorganJamesBOGO.com
2. Sign your name CLEARLY in the space
3. Complete the form and submit a photo of the entire copyright page
4. You or your friend can download the ebook to your preferred device

Morgan James BOGO™

A **FREE** ebook edition is available for you or a friend with the purchase of this print book.

CLEARLY SIGN YOUR NAME ABOVE

Instructions to claim your free ebook edition:
1. Visit MorganJamesBOGO.com
2. Sign your name CLEARLY in the space above
3. Complete the form and submit a photo of this entire page
4. You or your friend can download the ebook to your preferred device

---

Print & Digital Together Forever.

Snap a photo   Free ebook   Read anywhere

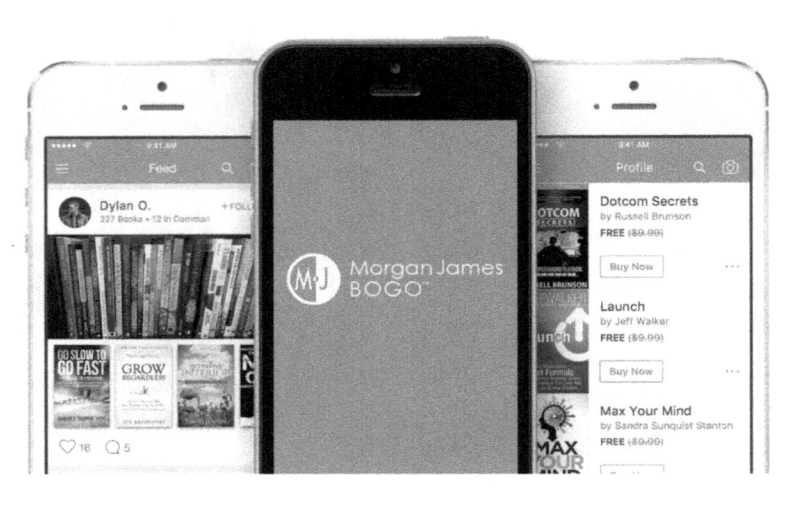

CPSIA information can be obtained
at www.ICGtesting.com
Printed in the USA
JSHW040325020421
13171JS00004B/16

9 781631 954405